"Am I Your Mother?"

Lynne LaForge Shane

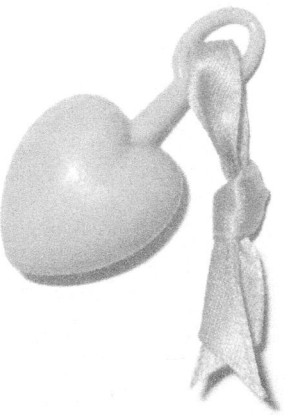

"Am I Your Mother?"

Independently Published
KDP Self-publishing
ISBN: 979-8-39-605493-6

Cover design and layout by
CAGEY DESIGN
cageydesign@gmail.com

GRA • DILSEACHT • CAIRDEAS  LOVE • LOYALTY • FRIENDSHIP

This book is dedicated to
my dear Mama

and

To Mothers everywhere...
the Caretakers of the world.

THANK YOU

Many people helped me with this book, not the least of whom was my Mama. I had been writing stories all of my adult life, happy and sad, funny and serious. Then the five years I cared for Mama in my home brought a wealth of new stories.

But as precious as those stories were to me, they never would have seen the light of day if it hadn't been for "a little help from my friends." Members of our writing group, my musician friends, visitors to my home, my family, all encouraged me to "publish my book."

But the one person who actually made that a reality - ink on paper - hold it in your hand, out into the world, is my very dear friend and graphic designer, Keith Glaseman. If it weren't for his expertise, the stories in this book would still be hidden in some obscure file on my computer or collecting dust in the bottom of a desk drawer.

Thank you, Keith.

(And a special "thank you" to my dear friend, Terri Robone, for her love and help to me and Mama through the years.)

INTRODUCTION

When I brought Mama from her home in Los Angeles, where she had been living for fifty years, to live with me in my log cabin in a remote mountain village, it was a big adjustment for both of us. Some days were difficult. Most days were wonderful. All days were a gift. My gift to her was obvious: I was able to care for her at a time in her life when she really needed me. But her gifts to me were life-changing. By her sweet and patient example, she showed me humor, gratitude, acceptance and love of family.

The existence of these stories is perhaps the most surprising gift of all. I have always seen myself as a parent, musician and teacher, rather than as a writer, but when Mama would say something so cute and funny, or tell me a story that touched my heart, I would think: I have to write that down. From that modest beginning has evolved this collection of stories that tell, not just about our life together, but also our history, our family, and the heart of us all, the lovely lady who was, and always will be, my Mama.

MY STORIES

THE OTHER LYNNE

I helped Mama back into her chair in the den, wrapped her in her afghan and put her oxygen back on. Then I went into the kitchen to make a cup of tea.

After a minute or so she started calling, "Is Lynne here?"

I said, "Yes, Mama, I'm here," but she kept calling over and over, "Is Lynne here? Did she go someplace? Is Lynne here?"

Finally, I went back into the den and said again, "Yes, Mama, I'm here."

Pointing to my vacant chair where I had left my rumpled afghan when I got up to help her, she said, "But Lynne must have gone someplace. Her chair's empty."

When I said, "Mama, I'm Lynne," she shook her head firmly. "No, I'm looking for the other Lynne."

I was sort of used to that by then, or as used to it as I could get. It was always a bit of a surprise when my own mother didn't know me. "I'm the only one who's here, Mama."

Thinking that I was the one who was confused, she gave me a consoling pat on the arm, smiled brightly and said,

"Well, that's all right! I like you better than that other one anyway!"

MIRROR, MIRROR, ON THE WALL...

A long-ago memory of when I was very young still makes me smile. I was sitting on the edge of the bathtub, watching Mama at the bathroom sink mirror putting on her makeup. I was so little that my feet didn't even reach the floor so I swung them back and forth, gently bumping my heels against the side of the tub.

Mama finished her makeup, brushed her lovely red hair, looked at herself carefully in the mirror one last time, and closed her cosmetic case. She turned to me with her wonderful smile and a twinkle in her eye, and said, "Well, I'd better stop now. If I get any more beautiful, the world won't be able to take me."

I was too young to understand her little joke. In my childish eyes, my Mama was the most beautiful lady in the world. I hopped down from the tub, ran over, threw my arms around her knees and said, "O.K. Mama, you can stop now."

The other day I was looking in the mirror over my bathroom sink. Decades have gone by now, bringing white hair and laugh lines. I was putting on face lotion when that old memory flitted through my mind, "Well, I'd better stop now..."

PICKING UP AFTER ANNIE

LIVING WITH MAMA

Our little black poodle dog, Annie, had a favorite toy that she played with often. In fact, it was the only dog toy she played with. The rubber was thin, fragile and faded, but Annie treated it so gently. She gave it careful little tosses in the air or held it in her paws and nudged it with her nose until she could coax a whisper of a squeak out of it.

That toy could be found most anywhere, under the table or behind the chair. I certainly didn't care, but Mama couldn't stand it. Despite her 83 years, she was a fastidious housekeeper to the end. Or at least I thought that was her motive for constantly picking up Annie's toy and putting it on the footstool in front of her chair.

But one evening as she was going through her bedtime routine, picking up her two-inch-high stack of carefully folded Kleenex, straightening the afghan on her chair one last time, and checking to make sure she had finished the last drop of her orange juice, she picked up Annie's toy from her footstool and started toward her bed. I couldn't help myself: I had to ask, "Mama, where are you taking that toy?"

She answered with a big smile, "Oh, this toy? Isn't it cute? I'm taking it to bed with me."

"But Mama," I said, laughing, "that's Annie's dog toy."

Mama got this very determined look on her face, like a little girl who's just been asked to share her new birthday presents and is having none of it, and said firmly, "Well not anymore, it's not. It's mine now."

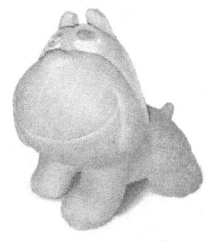

"Uncle" Bill

WE'RE ALL FAMILY

LIVING WITH MAMA

"Do you have any family?"

I glanced over at my 83-year-old Mama sitting in the passenger seat of the car. She had this bright-eyed smile on her face, waiting patiently for my answer.

Hmmm. What can I say? "Uh, family?"

Oblivious to my confusion, she replied, "Yes, you know, any brothers or sisters?"

I realized we were in another dimension, a place where time as we usually know it doesn't exist. Mama often lived outside the framework of clocks and calendars, but it still caught me off guard.

And I was reluctant to bring up the subject of my brother, because I didn't want to remind her that he had died, so I said rather tentatively, "Well, I had a brother, Jim."

"Jim, Jim? Why does that name sound familiar?"

I answered as gently as possible, "Mama, Jim was your son, and I'm your daughter, Lynne." Instead of looking confused or bewildered, her face lit up with delight. She clasped her hands in front of her like a little child and burst out, "Oh, how wonderful! That means we're all family!"

I nodded and smiled as she went on talking about her childhood. But to her, it wasn't in the past. It was then and there. She told me she had a wonderful brother named Bill, as if I had never known that before. Then she told me how handsome Bill was, and how he had gotten all the good looks in the family. At that point, I contradicted her and said, "I don't think that's so, Mama. You're just as pretty-looking a lady as Uncle Bill is a good-looking man. I don't think he got all the good looks."

She blushed at the compliment, tipped her head shyly to one side, and gave me a timid little smile. "Well, maybe that's so. My mother is a beautiful lady, and my father is a nice-looking gentleman, so I guess it would be natural for some of their good looks to rub off on us youngsters."

I looked again at my Mama, sitting there next to me. Her lovely white hair framed her beautiful face. Her complexion was smooth and glowing like silk. Her eyes twinkled and her smile was as sweet and gentle as the smile of a little child.

"Us youngsters?" Yes, I thought, I guess she is that. The years that separated our roles of mother and daughter had become blurred and faded, and the gap between generations had become unimportant. What was important was that we were, and are, as Mama said, "all family."

LYNNE BUM BIN

I was in the second grade when the teasing started. Kids at school would chant a taunting rhyme, using another kid's first name as the basis. Most of the girls in my class said they didn't like their names and wished they could change them, but I always liked my name and couldn't think of any name that I would like more than my own. That is, until my class-mates started ridiculing me. Then I wasn't so sure I liked it anymore.

When I got home and told Mama that the kids were making fun of my name, she said, "Well, what did they call you?" and I sang the limerick:

> *Lynne Bum Bin*
> *Tiddily In*
> *Tee-legged, Tie-legged*
> *Bow-legged Lynne*

Mama burst out laughing. "Well," she said, "some things never change, honey. Do you know what the kids in my school used to call me when I was a little girl?"

"What did they?" I asked, amazed that my grown-up Mama used to be a little girl like me.

And Mama sang her limerick:

> *Anna Banana*
> *Fee Fi Foe Fanna*
> *Tee-legged, Tie-legged*
> *Bow-legged Anna*

Then Mama and I were both laughing and she gave me a hug. I decided I really did like my name after all.

AM I YOUR MOTHER?

LIVING WITH MAMA

Paperwork! When I moved Mama from the family home in the city to my mountain cabin, I was overwhelmed with paperwork. In addition to learning the details of Mama's medical history, taking her to doctor appointments, obtaining her current medications and scheduling other necessary medical procedures, I also had to research and arrange for power of attorney, her will, and the sale of her home. I had no experience with any of these things, but family and friends helped out, step by step, and it seemed, page by page.

Our dear friend Terri went with Mama and me to act as a witness at the attorney's office where we needed to have legal documents drawn up. Terri and I were very concerned how the interview would go. One minute, Mama seemed to know who I was, and the next minute I was a complete stranger to her. Would she agree that I, her daughter, could handle her affairs and medical decisions?

We needn't have worried. Mama sailed right through without a hitch, telling the attorney that she wanted me, her "lovely daughter", to take care of her.

Then in the car on the way back to Terri's house, Mama leaned over, put her hand on my arm and said, "Honey, I want to ask you something."

"What, Mama?" I replied, eyes on the road.

"What I want to know, Honey, is, am I your mother?"

I glanced over at her worried face as she waited for my answer. "Yes, Mama, you're my mother and I'm your daughter, Lynne, and I love you, and I'm going to take care of you."

"Oh, good," she sighed, "I was hoping you would say that."

When we arrived at Terri's house, I left Mama there while I went back out to do errands.

Terri met me at the door when I returned. "Wait till I tell you what your Mama's been telling me," she said with a grin. "First, she wanted to know who that strange lady was who just left. That, my dear, was you, her 'lovely daughter' of half an hour ago. When I told her you were her daughter, she said, 'No, I've never seen her before.' I insisted you were her daughter, several times, and finally she said, 'Well, maybe she's my adopted daughter. She can't be my real daughter. She doesn't look anything like me. She doesn't have my red hair.'"

I'M NEVER GOING TO GET MY OWN NAIL POLISH

When I was a little girl, about six or seven, I bit my fingernails. Mama did everything she could think of to get me to stop, from bribing me with the prospect of clear, shiny nail polish of my very own, to threatening me with the suspension of every privilege I had, now or forever. I really wanted to stop biting my nails so I would grow up to have beautiful hands with red polish like Mama had, but somehow, I just couldn't seem to keep my fingers out of my mouth.

Finally, in desperation, Mama told me if I didn't stop my nail biting, she would sell me to the Armenians. I don't know where she got such a crazy idea. I doubt if she even knew anything about Armenians except that they lived in some faraway country. But parents in those days told their children horror stories like "Hansel and Gretel" where witches cook children in ovens, or "The Red Shoes" where the little girl ended up getting her feet chopped off for being so vain as to want red dancing shoes instead of sensible brown boots. So, I guess by comparison, selling your child to the Armenians was a rather mild punishment.

About this time, a young family moved into the apartment building where we lived; a handsome, dark-haired man; his pretty, petite wife; and their darling baby, a little boy of about six months with huge brown eyes and black curly hair. The father was an opera singer, and when he would practice his singing, we could hear him all over the building. We neighborhood children were all enchanted with his beautiful music, and the idea that a father could sing on stage for all those people was much more romantic than my father's job of working for the post office.

What we didn't know, but would soon find out, was that this lovely little family was Armenian. I can still remember my mother sitting down next to me, with a quiet, almost remorseful manner, taking my hand, looking sadly at my chewed-up fingertips, and saying softly, "Honey, there's something I have to talk to you about ..."

AREN'T WE LUCKY?

"I bet my mother misses me," Mama said, glancing over at me wistfully. Despite her 83 years, she looked like a sad little girl.

"She does? Where is your mother?" I asked, knowing full well that Grama Rae, Mama's mother, had died over fifty years ago.

"Oh, she's in Ohio. She gave me permission to come on this trip." Mama looked a little more cheerful.

"Where are you going on your trip?"

"To Michigan." As I was thinking about the distance between our mountain cabin in California and Michigan, she said, "I'm going to visit some of my father's family, but I'm so stupid I can't remember where they live."

"Mama, you're not stupid."

She brightened up at the compliment and looked quite happy. "No, I guess I'm not. I come from a very good home. I have a lovely mother and a good father and a pretty good brother."

"A pretty good brother?" This was the first time I had ever heard Mama call her brother, Bill, anything but wonderful.

"Yes, he's a pretty good brother. As long as he gets his way all the time, we get along just fine."

"Well, I guess some brothers are like that," I said, thinking of my only brother, Jim; handsome, charming, darling boy, gone now, way too young to lose him. Mama pulled me out of my reverie with her next declaration.

"No, I've decided I'm not stupid. I know how to count."

"You do?" I was used to those fast left turns.

"Yes, see up there above the radio?" She pointed to a row of small wooden boxes with bright colorful labels on the shelf over the television. (There's no radio.) "It says, 'One, two, three, four, five, six, seven, eight, nine, ten.'" She waved her arm up above her head and grinned triumphantly. The box labels had pictures of animals and titles like "Fido" and "Tom Cat" but no numbers; and there were only seven boxes.

Not knowing quite how to reply, I murmured, "Well, how about that."

"And," she held both her feet up in front of her, "I've got two perfectly good feet. Aren't I lucky?"

"Yes, you are." I guess that says it all. The wisdom of the ages. Aren't we lucky?

THE GOOD OLD DAYS

THE GOOD OLD DAYS

At the age of four, I came from back east to California with my parents. We moved to a place that no longer exists, The "poor" section of Beverly Hills. The apartment we lived in has long since been torn down, and any remaining homes or buildings in our old neighborhood have been renovated, remodeled and landscaped to fit their expensive addresses.

My Daddy worked for the Beverly Hills post office, and the United States government didn't believe in paying its employees much money back then, but a civil service job meant security, and, to a family man, security was everything.

I have fond memories of my early years in that apartment. As a young child, I knew nothing about being poor. I had everything a little girl could want: a beautiful mother who would take me downtown to Farmers Market for lunch, or to her favorite "hole in the wall" hamburger stand for burgers and fries. She bought me a beautiful yellow taffeta dress for the May procession, and protected me from the mean little boy who lived upstairs in our building. Even though Mama was very strict with me and did not spoil me, I felt safe and loved.

Her sternness was offset by my gentle father, who was as handsome as a movie star and twice as wonderful. He was kind and patient with me, and, although he worked long hours, he was always doing things for me. The other children in the neighborhood had stilts made of plain wooden stakes with wooden blocks nailed to the sides for footrests. Daddy made my stilts with footrests securely screwed in place, carefully sanded and beautifully painted a soft cream color.

When I started using pen and ink in school, we had the kind of pen with a split point that you dipped in the inkwell. Since I was left-handed, I tended to drag my hand through the wet ink, smearing my writing and staining the cuff of my sweater. While Mama complained about the ink stains, Daddy was the one who sat at the kitchen table with me, teaching me how to hold my hand under the line. He told me stories of when he was a little boy; the teachers didn't allow children to write with their left hand, and smacked their knuckles with a ruler if they forgot.

My parents couldn't afford to buy me a new bicycle, but Daddy got an old rusty one, sanded every square inch, painted it my favorite color (a beautiful shade of burgundy red), and had it waiting for me on Christmas morning! As young as I was, I recognized that it was a home-painted bike because the wheel rims were the same color paint as my stilts. But I liked it all the more because cream was a much prettier color with red than plain chrome like other bikes.

Our old apartment building looked rather charming from the outside. There was a huge jacaranda tree in front (we kids called it the bluebell tree), and a second-story balcony outside of the Parker's apartment. Mr. Parker, a war veteran, had an amputated leg, drove a special car with hand controls, and charged up the wide staircase to his second story apartment with his crutches two steps at a time. If he had packages that needed to be carried, Mrs. Parker would pay us kids a nickel for helping out. Then my Mama would scold me for taking the nickel, saying I should be doing the neighborly thing out of the goodness of my heart, a lofty motive for a little kid who didn't have a nickel to spend very often.

On the wall of the upstairs landing was a metal ladder leading to a trap door on the roof, where Mama would sometimes go to sunbathe in the summer. She came down one afternoon, all flustered, and told Daddy that she was lying up there top-less when a small airplane flew overhead, then turned around and flew over again. Daddy started laughing and Mama told him, "Stephen, stop that! It isn't funny!" But Daddy just laughed harder.

The inside of the apartment wasn't quite as charming as the outside however. When we first moved there, to a back apart-ment, our living room window looked out onto the clotheslines and the carport wall. Later we were able to move to a front apartment where the windows faced the front yard and street. There was a Murphy bed that folded down from the wall in the living room and wall sconces that didn't work; probably would have burned the place down because of that old wiring. The built-in dinette sat three if you pulled up an extra chair to the outside of the table, and the kitchen was only big enough to hold a stove and icebox (yes, an old-fashioned icebox) on one side, and a sink and a small cupboard on the other.

I felt important helping Mama in the kitchen with simple chores, setting the table, tearing lettuce for salad and mixing plain white oleo with powdered yellow food coloring and pressing it into a mold to make margarine cubes. Yuk! Mama always kept one cube of real butter on hand, saying that she was raised on a farm and we would have to be poorer than we were now not to have a little pat of butter on toast now and then. We had hot oatmeal every morning (I love hot oatmeal to this day), and on Sunday we put raisons in it. One day Mama was cooking lima beans in the new-fangled pressure cooker which overheated and sprayed beans all over the ceiling. Mama was not happy! And I never have liked lima beans ever since.

Then there was a long dark hallway that led to a tiny bathroom and one small bedroom which had the only closet in the entire place. I slept alone in that back room, while my parents sat in the front room, listening to late night radio programs like "The Shadow" and "Inner Sanctum," programs I wasn't allowed to hear because they "weren't suitable for children." Quietly, I would tiptoe down the hall to eavesdrop and then rush back to my bed when I got too scared, or when I thought Mama would catch me out of bed.

I'm not sure where I got the idea of being kidnapped, whether from those programs or from somewhere else, but once I got it stuck in my head, I couldn't get it out. There were two small windows in my bedroom that looked out on a narrow walkway bordered by a tall dense hedge. The screens on those windows were old and rusty and when I pressed on them, my finger went right through. I was convinced that a kidnapper could stick his finger through that hole, unhook the screen, climb in the window and steal me out of my bed. My sweet, patient Daddy bought wire and carefully repaired the holes in the screens, thinking to soothe my fears, but of course when I pressed on the screen again, it gave way. Daddy got out the wire again, planning to repair the screen one more time, but Mama had heard enough of my nonsense. She sat me down, and said sternly, "All right, I don't want to hear one more word about kidnapping. You are not going to be kidnapped. Only rich kids get kidnapped and we are poor!" And you know, that made perfect sense to me and I never worried about being kidnapped again.

[Ann, Lynne, Stephen]

COOKIES

In Mama's later years, all she wanted to eat was cookies, cookies, cookies. Forget all those wholesome, well-balanced meals she prepared for her family over the years. If it didn't have sugar in it or on it, she didn't want it. It had gotten so that I had to keep a careful eye on her while she ate, or she would give her whole meal to our dog, Annie.

During our visit to my hairdresser-friend Terri's house, where I took Mama each week to have her hair and nails done, Terri asked me if Mama would eat a tuna sandwich. "Well," I said, "some days she will and some days she won't."

I fixed a small plate: half a tuna sandwich with the crusts cut off, three spoonfuls of cottage cheese with lots of sugar, and a third of a banana, her favorite fruit. She took a couple of bites, announced she was full, and could Annie have the rest of her food? Then I went through the whole routine — coaxing, reasoning, and finally the guilt trip: "Mama, the doctor says if you don't start eating your food, you're going to end up in the hospital. You don't want to be in the hospital, do you?"

She straightened up her 95-pound self as indignantly as possible, banged her plate down on the table next to the couch, and said loudly, "Well, I guess I'll just have to go to the DAMN hospital, because I'm not eating this!"

Terri overheard her from the kitchen and came into the den, the corners of her mouth twitching, suppressing her laughter at my proper, lady-like mother actually using the word "damn." "Why, Ann," she said, in a sing-song Pollyanna voice, "how's your lunch? It looks like you're doing a good job of eating that sandwich."

With great disdain, Mama replied, "Well, I think so too, but they want me to eat this CRAP." It was too much. Two four-letter words in a row from my polite little Mama. And I guess I was the anonymous "they". Terri and I both burst out laughing, and Mama sat there with a satisfied smile on her face.

Shortly after that, Terri and I were down the hall in the hair salon, where Terri was cutting my hair. Her seven-year-old granddaughter, Amanda, who had been visiting that day, poked her head in the doorway, keeping her feet in the hallway, because she wasn't supposed to come in and interrupt while her Grandma was working.

"Grammersbee," she said, in that cute voice little kids use when they want to talk you into something fun.

"What, honey?"

"Grammersbee, the girl on the couch wants cookies."

LIAR, LIAR, PANTS ON FIRE

I have an old secretary-style desk in my bedroom that belonged to Mama. When she came to live with me in my mountain cabin, I brought it along with several other of her favorite pieces of furniture, including an oak storage chest with carved handles that belonged to Nini, my father's mother; a small pine cabinet to hold extra dishes; and a cream-colored triple-dresser that was part of a French Provincial bedroom set.

Mama had the mahogany desk painted a cream color to blend in with her new bedroom set, but, like many refinished furniture pieces, the top coat of light paint had chipped off here and there over the years, revealing the dark wood underneath.

By the time the desk survived the move to my house, it looked well-battered, and I thought, oh, well, someday I'll have it refinished. Then, several years later, I saw the same style desk in a catalogue of antique furniture. That desk was also painted, very chipped, had what the catalogue referred to as "an authentic patina," and the price tag was a cool $5,000.00! Well, heck, I guess I won't have my desk painted. I've grown to like its light color contrasting with my log cabin walls.

And besides, that desk has a history, just the way it is. Before I brought it up to my mountain cabin, it was in Mama and Daddy's home for fifty years, and before that, it was in our three-room apartment in the "poor" section of Beverly Hills. We had lived in that building for eight years and probably would have lived there much longer, but for the fact that the apartment was sold and all of the tenants were evicted in preparation for renovation.

I remember as a twelve-year-old girl listening to some man in our apartment, probably the new owner, talking loudly to my Mama, rudely opening cupboards, drawers and closets, and rummaging through our personal belongings. Then he opened up the desk and started yanking out papers, saying, "All this furniture belongs to the apartment, right?"

Mama had had enough of his bad manners and overbearing attitude. She spoke up indignantly, saying, "This desk doesn't belong to you. We brought this desk with us from Michigan." She took her papers right out of his hand and practically pushed that man out the door of the apartment.

Later that night, I overheard Mama saying to Daddy, "But Stephen, I don't care if it's ours or not. I couldn't stand that man for one more second. He was so rude." Daddy was probably pointing out the fact that although the desk was old and well-used, it wasn't actually ours, since we had come from Michigan to California in a two-door Chevy coupe, with just a few suitcases. No desk tied to the rooftop.

Mama and Daddy were both as honest as the day is long, but there are limits to what a person will put up with. Mama decided that desk belonged more to her after using it for eight years than it did to that rich man, who was probably going to trash it along with all the other old furniture in that old building. Whatever her reasoning, when we moved out of the apartment, she brought that desk with us to our new home in the suburbs.

On that desk today, I have a beautiful old fountain pen that belonged to Mama, a memento of all the years she enjoyed that desk. And there's a tiny wooden pink heart hanging from the knob of the small cabinet next to the letter slots. When I open that little door to take out stamps or address labels, I look at that heart and think, Mama loved this desk. It was her first piece of furniture. And I love it too.

BACK SEAT DRIVER

LIVING WITH MAMA

In the first year that Mama lived with me, she was in and out of the hospital nine times. She not only had dementia but also congestive heart failure, which caused frequent episodes of difficult breathing or chest pain. The local EMTs were on a first-name basis with us. If I met them in our village market, they would say, "Hi, Lynne, how's Ann doing today?"

When they came to the house to examine Mama, her symptoms would sometimes diminish, but, more often than not, I ended up following the ambulance to the hospital. If her condition didn't turn out to be too serious, we tried to make our trip into a pleasant outing, by stopping for take-out dinners from our favorite restaurant or buying ice cream cones or chocolate malts for the trip home.

I remember one trip we took, shortly after Mama had come to live with me. It was wintertime. Since I had only been living in the mountains myself for a few months, I had not yet purchased a four-wheel-drive car, a necessity for icy and snowy mountain roads. My son, Ken, was with me at the time, helping out with house repairs. He and Mama and I had all gone out early that morning to the hospital down in the valley to have Mama checked out because of chest pains. As usual, it took an extremely long time to wade through all the red tape and decide whether her condition was serious enough to keep her there overnight, or to let her come back home.

It was early evening before she was finally discharged, and we got underway. A storm was coming in, and as we left the valley and started up the mountain road, the wind picked up. Then it was pouring rain, and then it was snowing really hard. I couldn't see a thing except the snowflakes flying past the windows like the stars in the introduction to Star Wars.

Ken was hanging his head out the passenger window, trying to see the white line so we wouldn't end up in the road ditch. As I was creeping along on what I thought was the middle of the road, Ken suddenly hollered, "Uh Mom! The double yellow line's on my side!" Fortunately, there were no cars in the oncoming traffic lane, and I was able to slip and slide back over to the right side of the road again.

Then Ken and I got out and tried to put on chains. Oh! My! Gosh! We were still "city people" at that point, and didn't have any experience with chains. We also didn't have any gloves or weatherproof jackets. By the time we got the chains on and climbed back into the car, we were both frozen stiff. And I still had to make the icy, snowy trip ahead.

As I pulled out onto the road again, and Ken and I sat there, speechless, shivering and chattering, Mama spoke up from the back seat. "Well, what I want to know," she demanded in an irate voice, "is what are we doing out on a terrible night like this anyway?"

SLEEPWALKING

When I was twelve years old, my parents moved from our three-room apartment and bought their first, and only, home. They were so proud, happy and grateful to be homeowners. Our new place was basically a nice house in a pleasant, quiet neighborhood, but it had been sold at a reduced price as a fixer-upper, and it surely was that. Every square foot of it was scarred, scratched, battered and broken. Holes were punched in walls, windowpanes were cracked or missing, and cupboard doors were off their hinges.

But my folks didn't care. They started right in cleaning and repairing and making it our home. I have an amusing memory of tiptoeing down the hardwood floor in our new hallway, carefully staying to one side. Daddy had sanded, stained and varnished the other side of the floor, and it was still wet.

Each room was thoroughly cleaned, repaired as necessary, patched and painted. Paint in those days smelled terrible, and the fumes lasted for several days. So, when it was time to paint my bedroom, Mama made me a pallet of pillows and blankets on the floor next to their bed, where I could sleep away from the fumes.

The next morning when I woke up, Mama asked me if I had a dream the night before, and I said yes, and told her about it. In my dream, I got up out of my bed, walked down the long hall to the kitchen, opened an overhead cabinet, and took down a gold-foil box of Mama's chocolates. Just as I opened the box and picked up one of the candies, Mama came in the room and said, "Lynne, what are you doing?"

I answered, "I was just going to eat one of your chocolates."

Then Mama took the box away from me and said, "No, you can't have that," and made me go back to bed.

Mama had a strange look on her face when I finished telling her about my dream. She explained that I had gotten up during the night, walked over to my Daddy's closet, opened the door, and had taken a box down from the top shelf. When she woke up and saw me there, I was standing at the foot of their bed, with the box in one hand, and Daddy's loaded pistol in my other hand, pointing the gun at my face!

Mama and Daddy both agreed about the danger of having an unlocked loaded gun in the house. That gun was put away, out of sight, and I never saw it again.

LIFE IN A SMALL TOWN

LIVING WITH MAMA

"Who was that person we just drove past, Honey? They were waving at us." Mama turned in the passenger seat to look at the car going by us, on the quiet street in our small mountain village.

"I don't know, Mama. I haven't met them yet, but people here are just friendly, even to strangers like us."

It had taken me a bit of time to get used to such small-town neighborliness when I first moved here from the city. There, you never talked to strangers. You never looked a stranger in the eye. You kept a careful eye on your purse or wallet, and stayed out of deserted areas, especially at night. Those were the rules. That's what you did to stay safe. In the city.

But here, those rules went out the window. Neighbors went out of their way to talk to you. Shoppers in the little market smiled at you, and asked how you were doing. And, of course, drivers waved.

As Mama and I lived here longer, we discovered more ways in which people in this community cared for each other, including us. My friends Ron and Barbara, who were the only people I knew when I first moved here, had welcomed me with open arms, and introduced me to all their musician friends. When Mama came to live with me, a few months later, that circle of new friends helped me find medical professionals for Mama's care, music students I could teach at home, and eventually a whole network of young women and their mothers to help me with home care. My new neighbors invited us to their homes for dinners, book studies and watching movies. They drove us to community events, outings to see the poppies, and four-wheel-drive trips to admire the view from the top of the mountain.

I had never lived in an area that had four seasons before. But this was southern California, so in the mountains those four seasons are mild and lovely. In the springtime, the wildflowers cover the hillsides with radiant color, and in the summer, the not-too-hot days are a welcome escape from the heat and humidity of the valleys. The trees change color in the fall, brilliant reds and golds mixing with the dark green of the pines. Then when the winter snow comes, usually just enough to look beautiful, we are rewarded by glittering icicles hanging from the porch roof, snowflakes decorating every tree as if for Christmas, and the breath-taking view of the snow-capped mountain tops. I love it all.

One afternoon, Mama and I drove out to get a few groceries and pick up a prescription at the local pharmacy. As we were parked on the quiet street, right in the center of the little town, mind you, I saw our friend Ron driving towards us. He stopped in the middle of the street, rolled down his truck window, and started talking to us. Occasionally another car came along, slowed down, then casually drove around Ron's truck and went on their way. And Ron just kept talking, evidently not noticing the other cars at all. I was a little surprised, but mostly amused, by this example of the friendly, comfortable, unhurried pace of life in a small town.

TOY SOLDIER

LIVING WITH MAMA

"O.K., Mama, now I'll be right back," I said, as I tucked the afghan around her feet. "I'm just going over to pick up Michele."

"O.K., honey," Mama answered. "I'll wait right here for you."

Michele was one of Mama's favorite home-care girls. This group of young women and their mothers enabled me to run errands without always having to bring Mama with me, along with her oxygen tanks and wheelchair. Thanks to these wonderful helpers, Mama was able to stay comfortably at home with a new friend to visit, and I was able shop quickly and efficiently, or sometimes just have some time to myself.

I made sure Mama's orange juice glass was full and her tissue box was nearby. She had just used the bathroom, so she wouldn't have any reason to get up from her chair in the den while I was gone. Our little dog, Annie, hunkered down at her self-appointed post on Mama's footstool, wagging her tail. As I went out the door, I said again, "I'll be right back," and Mama answered again, "I'll wait right here for you, honey."

Michele's house was close by, and she was ready when I pulled into her driveway. I didn't even have to stop the car engine as she came hurrying out.

She gave me her warm smile, and we chatted about her school and my errands and other small talk on our way back to the house.

When we walked in my front door, I stood frozen with shock in the entry hall, staring into the den. Mama was lying flat out on the floor, not moving a muscle. I might have thought she was dead, except for the fact that her entire body was perfectly rigid. Her arms were straight down beside her with the palms pressed against the side of her thighs. Her legs were right together with the toes of her Uggs pointing up at the ceiling.

Even her head was straight, chin up, eyes looking at the ceiling fan. She happened to be dressed in a long-sleeved red velour top and plain black pants, and she looked for all the world like a wooden toy soldier.

As Michele and I stood there staring, both of us completely speechless, Mama very slowly turned her head to face us, gave us a big smile, and said very calmly, "Hi honey, I'm waiting right here for you."

BEAUTY BEFORE AGE

"I'm so tired of licking envelopes, Mama. Can't we quit now?"

"I'm tired too, honey, but we're almost done, ...just a few more."
Mama gave a little groan as she straightened up in her chair.
We were sitting on uncomfortable folding chairs at a card table
in the eating area of our new house. You really couldn't call it
a dining room because it was such a small space, only a little
wider than a hallway leading from the front living room back
to the kitchen.

Mama and I were working at an at-home clerical job, a
common practice for stay-at-home housewives in those days.
My part was to fold preprinted letters or flyers, insert them
into envelopes, lick them closed, yuck, put on a stamp which
also had to be licked, and pass them over to Mama. She was
addressing the blank envelopes with her beautiful handwriting
from a list supplied by her employer. Then she would repack the
envelopes back into their boxes, send them to the post office
with Daddy to be mailed, and arrange to receive more boxes of
flyers, envelopes, stamps and mailing lists. It was a seemingly
endless, boring, low-paying job, but necessary for us.

You see, the payment on our new home, new to us that is,
was more than the rent on our old apartment from which we
had recently been evicted, along with all the other tenants.
With a small loan from my Mama's family, which was carefully
paid back month by month, my parents were able to purchase
a "fixer-upper" for $5,000. That sounds incredible by today's
standards, but back then it was a great deal of money on a
mail-carrier's salary. Our house was in dire need of repair, and
even modest supplies like paint, sandpaper and window glass
were an extra expense for us. We also had almost no furniture,
having come from a furnished apartment.

We had moved too far away for Mama to go to her previous part-time job as a switchboard operator. So now we were stuck with at-home jobs — but not for long.

Mama had plans. She was a very intelligent, talented and disciplined woman. She used to tell me that when she was growing up her brother was the scholar in the family. He always got all "A's" but she got "B's" in arithmetic. Well, that still meant that she got "A's" in everything else, and she turned that fine mind of hers to acquiring new skills. She signed up for at-home classes in typing, bookkeeping, and a new type of shorthand called "speedwriting." I remember her showing me how to speedwrite and how much fun I had with it.

Not too much time went by before Mama felt ready to look for a new job. Looking back, it's really impressive how she juggled the responsibilities of caring for our home (no modern appliances like vacuum cleaners), laundry (done in a wringer washer and hung on the clothesline), ironing (no perma-press in those days), my four-year-old brother, Jimmy (who was always a handful), meals (all made from scratch; no convenience foods), our envelope-stuffing job, and still found time to study secretarial skills. Even as a kid I was proud of her. I didn't mind pitching in to help her with the housework and cooking, but I sure hated stuffing those damned envelopes. Oops, I wouldn't have said "damn" when I was a kid.

So now Mama started reading the "Help Wanted" ads in the newspaper and she found an advertisement that read as follows:

Wanted

For position of secretary
Female, age 25 to 32, white,
attractive, well-dressed
Experienced dealing with the public
Competent with all secretarial skills
College graduate preferred
Inquire at address below

I don't think they could run an ad like that today. It was the epitome of discrimination on so many levels. But standards were different back then.

Mama decided she was going to try out for that job. The location was close to home and she felt qualified on most of the listed requirements. The "well-dressed" part was a little worrisome as her wardrobe was very limited, but Mama had a great sense of style and looked good even in simple clothes, accenting them with just the right scarf or piece of jewelry. She felt that the college "preference" could be dealt with. Her prospective employer didn't need to know that her college training was in nursing and her secretarial training was at home in her bedroom at her own desk.

But the biggest concern was her age. A "college graduate" was unlikely to have a 14-year-old daughter before the age of 32. Mama was close to 40 at the time but looked very young for her age and could easily pass for 32 or even younger. So, she decided to do what most women did at that time: lie about her age. It wasn't really lying, you see, since everyone knew women over the age of 21 never admitted their real age. After talking over the requirements of the job with Daddy and me, she gave me a mischievous wink and said, "Well, honey, we're just going to have to keep you hidden in the attic."

Mama got the job. The company she went to work for was a prestigious real estate firm that dealt with multi-million-dollar properties. After a short time she was promoted to office manager, which was no surprise to us. We knew what Mama could do when she set her mind to it. She kept the whole place running like a Swiss watch. Everyone who worked there loved her, especially her boss. He turned out to be a really nice guy, despite his newspaper advertisement.

One summer, about two years after she was hired, her boss invited everyone from the company and their families to his home for a barbeque and swim party. He lived in a ritzy neighborhood in a large expensive mansion, complete with beautifully landscaped gardens and a large backyard pool. I remember being very excited. Just think, someone rich enough to have their very own pool!

Mama and I went shopping for a swimsuit and beach towel for me, especially for the occasion. Mama didn't need a swimsuit. She didn't swim. Actually, she didn't let anyone see her with wet, dripping hair and running mascara, especially not her boss.

When Mama, Daddy, Jimmy and I arrived at the party, a maid in a black uniform with a white apron answered the door and escorted us through the house to the patio out back. We walked over to greet our host. He already knew Mama had a husband who worked for the post office and a six-year-old son, but he knew nothing about me. I was 16 years old by then, as tall as Mama and with a young woman's figure. Imagine his surprise as Mama put her arm around my shoulders and said, "Sir, I'd like to introduce you to my lovely daughter, Lynne."

[My "Mama"]

THESE NEW-FANGLED GADGETS

LIVING WITH MAMA

My used-but-new-to-me Jeep has so many modern conveniences that I've never had in a vehicle before: electric locks, seats, and windows; digital display for temperature, compass, clock, and calendar; a CD player; and four-wheel drive. I even have the ultimate luxury: thick, honey-colored, warm-in-winter-cool-in-summer sheepskin seat covers.

I remember the day I bought them. Mama and I went to a small shop located on a busy boulevard, with a small parking lot in the back. I found a space under a huge shady tree, opened all the electric windows a bit for ventilation, told Mama I would be right back, locked the car with my new handy-dandy remote, and hurried into the store.

The shop was empty of customers and I had already decided on the color and style of seat covers I wanted, so it was only a couple of minutes before the salesman and I went back out to the parking lot to measure the seats. As we walked out the back door, we could hear a car alarm blaring and the salesman asked me if I had an automatic car alarm. Being oblivious to all the features of my new vehicle, I naïvely told him I didn't.

When we walked up to the Jeep, there was Mama, sitting in the passenger seat with her door partly open, looking very upset and confused, with the car alarm honking full volume. I didn't even know how to shut the alarm off, but fortunately the salesman did. As Mama was explaining to me that she was only trying to get some fresh air when "those people" started honking at her, the young salesman was obviously very amused at the whole situation, probably wondering which of these two old ladies was more confused. He said with a big grin, "You know, lady, I think you do have a car alarm."

A BAD HAIR NIGHT

Mama and I were sitting together one evening in the den when she started in with an old complaint, "Don't you think you ought to comb your hair?"

I inwardly groaned to myself, *here we go again*, but I said as patiently as I could, "It's practically bedtime, Mama. I don't care if it's combed."

"But you're so pretty. You'd look even prettier if you'd comb your hair."

"Mama, I'm just sitting around in my nightgown watching TV. I don't care if my hair's combed."

"Well, I care. You'd look much better with your hair combed."

"Please let's stop talking about my hair."

"I'll stop talking about it if you'll comb it."

"I'm not going to get up and go comb my hair. Let's just watch TV."

"You could watch TV with your hair combed."

"I don't want to talk about my hair anymore."

"OK. I won't talk about it." Ten seconds went by. "When I was a little girl, my mother brought me up right, and she taught me to comb my hair."

"I thought we weren't going to talk about combing hair."

"Well, you don't have to talk about it, but I want to talk about it."

"Mama, if you don't stop nagging me about my hair, I'm going to go sit in the other room."

"Oh no, no! I don't want you to go in the other room. I love you too much for you to be in the other room."

"OK, then."

"I'd love you even more with combed hair."

"Mama!"

"OK. I'll shut up." Ten more seconds went by. Then Mama looked at Annie. "Look at this cute little dog sitting here with me. She looks like she's got her hair combed."

About that time, I was trying not to burst out laughing. "No more talking about hair."

"OK." Ten seconds. "If you'd just comb..."

"NO talking about hair!"

"OK. OK." One whole minute went by. "Lynne?"

"Yes?"

"Would you bring me a cookie?"

"Yes, Mama. I'll get it in just a minute." I was busy scribbling down this conversation.

"You know what?"

"What, Mama?" I was still writing.

"You're not a selfish lady after all."

"I'm not?" Then I was laughing.

"No, and you're not ornery at all, like I first thought you were. You're a sweet lady now."

"I'm glad you think so." I guess daughters who bring cookies are sweet, even if they have messy hair.

"I'm sure lucky I met up with someone as nice as you."

"Well, I'm lucky I 'met up' with you too, Mama. I'll go get your cookies."

NEITHER SNOW NOR RAIN
NOR GLOOM OF NIGHT...

Some years ago, after Daddy was gone, I was going through my parent's papers, and I came across Daddy's application for admission to a school for artists. It was so delightful to see his drawings: the trees on the hillside, the cabin by the stream, the wildflowers bending over by the water's edge. You could almost smell the flowers and hear the water splash.

Daddy never did become a professional artist. He worked for the post office his entire career, a secure, steady job to take care of his family. We were always his first priority before anything he may have wanted for himself.

However, his artistic talent showed up in other ways, designing and drawing. His ideas of automobile design were radically different from anything on the road at that time. To his mind, the early box-shaped cars and the later huge boats-on-wheels were not aerodynamic, and so he designed cars that were small and streamlined, the type of automobile we see on our highways and freeways by the millions today.

Also, Daddy was observant. He saw problems with malfunctioning tools, cars or appliances as opportunities to find solutions. We had an old-style refrigerator, of course, the kind that stood up on legs and had a tiny little freezer that became encrusted with a thick layer of ice in an inconveniently short period of time. Daddy watched Mama defrosting that fridge, wrapping the frozen food in towels to keep it from melting, chipping away at the icy buildup literally with hammer and chisel, chunks of ice flying out and melting all over the kitchen floor. He knew there must be a better way. So, he invented a self-defrosting refrigerator! He attached a timer to the power cord which turned off the electricity during the night, just long enough to allow one day's accumulation of ice to melt into a pan under the refrigerator, and then turned the power back on before morning.

Unfortunately, Mama didn't appreciate Daddy's ingenuity and told him she had no intention of getting down on her hands and knees and emptying a tray of dirty water from under the refrigerator each morning. And so, since Daddy had to be at work at 4:00 a.m., he got down on his hands and knees and emptied the tray himself, at 3:00 a.m. Then he invented a way to fasten the tray to the underside of the refrigerator near the motor so the heat evaporated the water each day. I think Daddy could have made money with that invention, but it was reward enough for him to make Mama's life a little easier.

In addition to designing automobiles and inventing more efficient refrigerators, Daddy was also talented in woodcarving and woodworking. He made beautiful custom rifle stocks and designed and built most of the furniture in my childhood bedroom.

Years later, remembering the things Daddy had made for me, I coaxed him into drawing some pictures to decorate my young children's bedroom. He was in the beginning stages of dementia at that time and was starting to have hand tremors. He protested that he wasn't skilled enough to draw pictures suitable for framing, but of course he was, and the pictures are wonderful. They now hang in my hallway and I treasure them to this day. They are a lasting memento of a loving father who would do anything for his love of his family.

"Neither snow nor rain nor heat nor gloom of night, stays these couriers from the swift completion of their appointed rounds."

(From an ancient Greek work describing the Persian system of mounted postal carriers c. 500 B.C.)

(The United States Postal Service does occasionally cancel deliveries in unsafe weather conditions.)

IT'S THE LITTLE THINGS THAT MATTER

"Ken, would you please get some scissors and trim this ragged edge off?" Mama very carefully held up a torn piece of Kleenex, as if it were a delicate lace handkerchief.

My son, Ken, was totally perplexed. "You want me to trim that?"

"Yes, please honey, so it looks, you know, nice and straight on the edge." Mama looked up at him, innocently, smiling trustfully.

"Well, O.K. Grama, but..." He was smiling then, too. "How 'bout if I just get you another one?" He hopped out of his chair, got a fresh tissue, and handed it to her.

"Oh, honey, thank you." Mama looked up at Ken, delight and gratitude written all over her face. Then she held the new tissue up in front of herself, admiringly. "This is just lovely."

[My "Daddy"]

THE HUNTER

I have a charming black-and-white photograph of my Daddy that I found in Mama's desk years ago. He was probably in his late twenties when it was taken, maybe around 1940. At that time, the measure of a man's good looks was "tall, dark, and handsome," and Daddy was all of those things and more. Clark Gable was a very popular movie star at the time—you know, Rhett Butler in "Gone with the Wind"—and my Daddy resembled him, but in looks only. That's where the similarity ended. Instead of being a rascal like many of Clark Gable's movie characters, my Daddy was a hard-working, kind, loving husband and father. He was a gentleman in the finest meaning of that word.

In the photograph, taken in rural Michigan, Daddy is wearing a brimmed cap, old-fashioned breeches and knee-high boots. He is holding a rifle in one hand and a brace of pheasants in the other, with our black-and-white cocker spaniel, Skippy, standing at his feet. It's a rather romantic picture, in a way: the brave hunter, providing food for his family. But that wasn't really the motive for most men in that time and place, or here and now for that matter. Hunting was a sport, a measure of a man's skill and accuracy with a gun. A man's sport, away from the home, from the women and children, from the trappings of the city.

After we moved from Michigan to California, to Beverly Hills and later to West Los Angeles, Daddy would work in our garage in his spare time making custom rifle stocks. I remember how he would apply ink on the rifle barrel, set it gently into the unfinished stock, and then carefully chisel and sand away the high places, fitting the barrel into the stock again and again until it was perfect. Then he would design patterns for the outside, carving, sanding and staining the wood until it seemed to glow from the inside out. Those stocks were works of art. I used to spend time out there with him, working on my orange-crate doll house, making each piece of furniture by hand out of wood, using Daddy's tools. It was our time together, and it was precious to me.

Occasionally, on a weekend, Daddy would go out to the desert to hunt rabbits. One time when I was about fifteen, I begged him to take me with him. Mama was very much against it, and Daddy usually did what Mama thought best with my brother and me. But for some reason he insisted that I was old enough to go along. Looking back to that time, I think Daddy considered it our time together, and it was precious to him too.

We got up very early in the morning, way before dawn, dressed in our warm "hunting clothes," brought our packed lunch, and made the long drive to an unpopulated area of the desert. I was very excited to be on an outing with my Daddy, just the two of us.

We sat waiting quietly for quite a long time before the rabbits started coming out of their burrows. Then Daddy had a clear shot, raised his rifle and fired. We hurried over to where the rabbit was lying on the ground and stood there looking at it. The helpless little creature was not dead. It was on its back. Its abdomen had been ripped open, and intestines were spilled out everywhere. But the thing I remember most was the look on that little rabbit's face. It was staring up at us, its eyes wide with terror and agony. Pathetic little noises seemed to be pleading with us. Daddy said, in a voice I had never heard him use before, "Oh hell, I hate it when that happens." He told me to leave, and as I turned and started to run back towards the car, I heard another rifle shot, and knew he had quickly put the rabbit out of its misery.

I don't remember much more about that day. I think I was in a state of shock. Back in the car I just sat there, staring out the windshield. I couldn't talk, I couldn't cry. I couldn't seem to even think. When we got back home, I went in my bedroom, shut the door, threw myself on my bed, and buried my face in the pillow. I spent the whole weekend in my room, sleeping or staring out the window. Once I overheard Mama saying, "I told you it wasn't a good idea to take her," but Daddy didn't even answer her. He went out in back towards the garage, slamming the door behind him. For once Mama didn't get after me to do chores or even come out for meals. She seemed to know I needed to be alone.

Daddy told me later that he was sorry about the rabbit, sorry for hurting me, sorry for everything. I told him I was fine; I knew he didn't mean for things to turn out the way they did, and I loved him. We never talked about that day again.

But Daddy never went hunting again either, not alone and not with his friends who were hunters. He still made beautiful rifle stocks and visited with men who admired his work, but I don't think he ever again shot one of those rifles. Maybe he stopped seeing them as works of art, and started looking at them as instruments of suffering and death. Maybe he saw them through the eyes of a fifteen-year-old girl.

TV CRITIC

For Mama, the characters we saw on the TV shows and movies were the real deal. I don't think she realized they were actors playing fictitious roles but, even if she did, thinking they were real made her enjoy them more.

Her favorite hero was Cordell Walker, star of Walker, Texas Ranger. He saved the damsels in distress, usually at the last perilous moment, and knocked out the bad guys with some really impressive martial arts. I have to admit that I liked the show too, despite the exaggerated heroics.

At the end of every program, without fail, Mama would turn to me, hold up one finger, and say, "Honey, I'm going to tell you something."

"What's that, Mama?" I would reply, knowing exactly what was coming.

"That," and she would point to Walker's picture on the TV screen, "That is a good man."

And I would always answer, "I think so, too, Mama." Knowing a bit about the real Walker, Chuck Norris, and his code of ethics, I actually do think so, too.

Mama was not always approving of movie and TV stars, however. No matter how famous they might be, Mama had her own code of ethics about how they should behave.

In the movie Pretty Woman, the rich businessman is staying in an exclusive hotel, and the manager is explaining to him, as discreetly as possible, that the "lady" accompanying him is of questionable occupation, and is inappropriately dressed for this conservative establishment. Julia Roberts, who plays the part of the prostitute, is dressed with her boots up to here and her skirt up to there, and is definitely a stand-out in the crowd.

At the end of that show, Mama turned to me, held up one finger and said, "Honey, I'm going to tell you something."

"What's that, Mama?" I started laughing. This time, I wasn't sure what she was going to say.

"That," and she pointed to Julia on the TV screen, "that woman may be pretty, but she definitely is **no lady**."

LUNCH AT LYNNE'S

LIVING WITH MAMA

> Every Thursday at Noon
> Bring a Dish for the Potluck
> Bring Something to Read

Outings with Mama were time-consuming and required a lot of planning and effort. Getting Mama dressed and fed and then packing clothes, supplies, oxygen tanks and the wheelchair took up half of the day. It was much easier to stay home as much as possible, but then we missed visiting with friends and family as often as we would like. That's how "Lunch at Lynne's" came about.

It started with just one friend coming for a cup of tea, but that friend brought another friend and then it was lunch. Soon more friends brought dishes to share until it became a regular get-together. Mama and I were delighted. We had an occasion to dress up a bit, set the table with the good dishes and prepare a special recipe. Well, actually I was the one who did the preparations, but Mama enjoyed everything right along with me.

When lunchtime arrived, Mama would be sitting in her chair in the den, which adjoined our big kitchen, ready to greet our guests. Always the gracious hostess, she welcomed everyone with smiles, handshakes and hugs. She told all the ladies how pretty they looked and complemented them on their outfits, and although they might have been a bit embarrassed by the attention, they couldn't help but feel good too.

Mama never wanted to sit at the table with us; she preferred to stay in her chair nearby. When I fixed a small plate of food and brought it over to her, she would comment on how pretty the dishes were. I don't think she remembered they were often her own good china but she really appreciated them. And I think she liked the dishes more than the food, because she would just pick at all the unfamiliar items on her plate, pushing them around with her fork like a little kid.

In addition to enjoying each other's company and all the delicious food, my friends and I started bringing things to read aloud. Jean was the oldest member of our group and it was endearing to see and hear that beautiful white-haired lady reading letters that her mother had written to her when she was a young girl away in boarding school, a glimpse into a past way of life, long gone. Many other talented writers shared a meal and a story with us over the years, and it was here in the loving and supportive company of my dear friends that I read my first stories about Mama.

Although I had been writing essays and journals for years, I never thought about publishing a book. I am the mother of six grown children, many of whom now have children of their own. When I lived in the city, I had a large music clientele, teaching six acoustic stringed instruments: guitar, banjo, mandolin, dobro, hammered dulcimer and piano, playing traditional, old-time and Celtic music, and performing with several different groups. After I moved to the mountains, I took on a few new students, joined a local band and led a Celtic session each week. I even took up the concertina. So, of course, I saw myself as a mother and a musician.

But thanks to my dear "Lunch at Lynne's" friends who liked my stories, the many talented writers who encouraged me along the way, and of course Mama, who started it all, I began to write this book.

HIGH HEELS

LIVING WITH MAMA

One afternoon Mama and I went through an old scrapbook of her school days, looking at pictures of her as a young girl, tattered football pennants and faded dance cards. On a page titled "My Best Friend" she had pictures, not of her schoolmates, but of her own dear mother, whom she often referred to as her best friend.

She told me that one time she won $100.00 in a beauty contest for "Best Legs." How we laughed over that. When I asked her what she did with the money, she told me she put it in the bank, but soon after that, her mother became very ill and needed an operation. The family didn't have enough money to cover the medical expenses so Mama helped out with her $100.00.

I'm not surprised Mama could win a beauty contest. She was a beautiful woman and always dressed in stylish clothes and high-heeled shoes to show off her petite figure and beautiful legs.

When she was in her eighties, she was still walking around her house in her high-heeled slippers.

The first time I brought Mama up to the mountains to my cabin, it had snowed the night before and everything looked like a winter wonderland. But my driveway had three inches of fresh powder, and of course Mama couldn't walk from the car to the front porch with open-toed high-heeled slippers.

I ran in the house and grabbed my knee-high Uggs, and brought them back out to her. Fortunately, we wore about the same size shoe, and they fit her pretty well. After I helped Mama indoors and got her settled in a comfortable chair, I bundled her up in afghans and turned the pellet stove on to high. I made us some tea, and we waited for the chilly house to warm up.

Mama was a little upset, being in a strange place. She wanted to go home. Trying to distract her with something familiar, I brought over her high-heeled slippers and asked her if she wanted to change into them. She looked at my Uggs that I had put on her and then at her slippers, and shook her head. "No, honey," she smiled. "I like these new slippers you gave me just fine."

GRAMPA CAME TO VISIT

We got our first television set when I was fifteen years old. All of our friends and neighbors already had TVs, but Mama was dead set against it, because she said we would stop talking to each other and just sit around staring at the screen. That was a pretty accurate prediction, wasn't it? If not for our family, at least for society in general. But then we didn't end up getting our TV the way most people got TVs.

A couple of months before, my grandparents had been out to visit from Ohio. Even though my Grampa owned a successful business, and could have easily afforded to stay in a hotel or motel, he insisted on staying with us in our small home for their two-week visit. He said, "That's what families are for," and whatever he said, that's what everyone did. So, my parents gave up their bedroom with the double bed, and moved into my bedroom with the three-quarter-sized bed. I slept on a blanket on the floor in my brother's room, and although I didn't mind, (stuff like that is fun when you're a kid), my Mama certainly did mind.

But not because of Grama. My Mama adored her mother, and had told me many times that Grama was her best friend. After seeing them together during their summer visits, I could see why. I thought she was the best Grama that a kid could have, too. She was very short, only about as tall as I was, and very plump. Her long, pretty white hair was twisted around and pinned on top of her head in a bun, and she wore dark grandmother-type dresses with white lace collars that she crocheted herself.

Oh, and she baked delicious things too, especially pies. I can still remember her cherry pie. In my log cabin where I live today, I still have my Grama's ceramic pie dish, and every now and then I bake a cherry pie... using Grama's recipe, of course.

But my favorite thing that my Grama did for me was to make me doll clothes for the doll that I kept at the head of my bed, propped up on my pillows. It was an old-fashioned type of doll, and Grama designed a charming little red dress with embroidered trim and a red-and-white pinstriped pinafore to match, all made by hand with her tiny perfect stitches, since we didn't have a sewing machine.

[Grama & Grampa Dannemiller]

My Grampa was another matter. He was gruff and distant, ignoring my childish chatter by burying his head in the newspaper, or telling me to go outside and play. However, he often took us out for dinner, and that was a big adventure, not only because we seldom went out to eat, but because we all got to ride in his Cadillac convertible. Every few years, he would buy a new Cadillac, and then drive with Grama on a summer vacation. Riding in the back seat with my long curls blowing around my face was better than a rollercoaster ride at Disneyland. (Except Disneyland didn't actually exist at that time.)

On one particular occasion we were all dressed up, and went to a very nice restaurant. The maître d' met us at the door, and informed my Grampa, who was wearing a nice sport shirt and a cardigan sweater, that this was a "suit and tie" restaurant only. Then he reached over and took a necktie off a rack and tried to hand it to my grandfather. Well, Grampa was having none of that, let me tell you. He called over a pretty young waitress who was standing nearby, took out his wallet, pulled out a $100 bill (which was a lot of money in those days), and said, "Young lady, this would have been your tip if you had waited on me, but I'm giving it to you anyway." Then he glared at the maître d', turned on his heel and marched out the door. We all followed him, speechless, got back in the Cadillac, and drove to another nice restaurant that didn't require neckties.

I'm sure Grampa loved us, but he had a different way of showing it, and everything had to be his way. He had that Old-World mentality that a man is the king of his castle, and wherever Grampa was, that was his castle. Mama didn't take kindly to being bossed around, especially in her own home. To tell the truth, Grampa was probably one of the reasons that

Mama had moved to California—well, that and the weather; she hated those cold Ohio winters. Now she felt like he had tracked her down and she was under his thumb again.

He complained about the way she dressed (too modern), the way she cooked (or didn't cook), the fact that she hated sewing, and the way she kept house, a completely unfounded criticism in Mama's immaculate home. But the thing Grampa was most adamant about was smoking. Grampa declared that decent ladies did not smoke, and if Mama ever took up smoking, he would disown her, a considerable threat since he was worth a lot of money. Mama was so independent that I don't think she cared much about the money itself. But although she would defend herself against his other complaints, she never said anything one way or the other about smoking. You see, Mama had smoked cigarettes for years, and supposedly Grampa didn't know anything about it. The problem was, during their two-week visit, Mama just couldn't quit.

We only had one bathroom, and if Grampa wanted to go in there and someone else was inside, he would bang on the door, and yell for them to hurry up and get out. Sometimes the "someone else inside" was Mama, who had gone in to sneak a cigarette. She would open the bathroom window, spray her perfume around, flush the empty toilet, and come out with an innocent smile on her face. As a kid, I was incredulous, watching this little scenario play out. Anybody with half a brain could see and smell the cigarette smoke hanging in the air, but Grampa always acted as if he didn't notice. It didn't make a bit of sense to me, but before I could give anything away, my Daddy took me aside and explained that Mama really loved her father, despite his tyrannical ways, and didn't want to openly defy him. And

Grampa, for all his gruffness and complaining, really loved Mama and didn't want to disown her. He just wanted to seem to be the boss.

At the end of their visit, Grampa told us he was sending us an early Christmas present, and not to go out and buy ourselves anything big, like a piece of furniture or something. Daddy and Jimmy and I were pretty excited, because we thought maybe we were getting a television set, but Mama said we'd better not be, because Grampa knew she was set against us having one.

Well, sure enough, a short time later, a big, heavy carton arrived from Grampa and Grama, with an accompanying letter to Mama, saying they hoped we wouldn't spend all our time sitting in front of it. I can still remember the sight of that beautiful mahogany cabinet as Daddy pried off the cardboard lid. But when he opened the front of that carton, we stared in astonishment. It was a sewing machine! Never, ever, before or since, have I seen my mother act like she did that day. She always had, as Daddy affectionately called it, a red-headed personality, but that day it was nothing short of a teen-aged temper tantrum. Yelling and hollering, she stormed up and down the hallway slamming doors, all the while complaining at the top of her voice that her father never was happy with her, never accepted her for who she was, and always wanted her to be someone she was not. She told us, as if we didn't know, that she hated sewing, was never going to sew a stitch on that sewing machine, and was never even going to sew on another button if she could help it. I have to say to my mother's credit that throughout her tirade she was still a lady, never using "bad language," as they used to say in those days.

However, the very next day, Mama and Daddy went out shopping and brought home a television set in a handsome mahogany cabinet. I never did quite figure out Mama's reasoning for that decision; sort of a back-handed defiance against her father somehow. But whatever the reason, Mama became a real TV fan, setting aside time in the evenings to watch her favorite shows.

And the sewing machine? Well, true to her word, Mama never touched it. But it was way too nice a piece of furniture to put out in the garage, which is where she probably would have preferred to put it. So, it ended up in a far corner of their bedroom, with things stacked on top of it and boxes stored underneath it. When I married a few years later, Mama gave me, among other lovely gifts, that same sewing machine. Although I've never been much of a seamstress, I taught myself to sew simple patterns, making baby clothes and little girl's smocked dresses and matching mother-daughter outfits. I had many happy hours at that machine, and much satisfaction dressing my little ones in clothes I had made with my own hands.

But my favorite memory of that machine is of a long-ago summer day when I was still a teenager. My Mama and my brother Jimmy were out somewhere, and I was home alone with my Daddy. He called me to come down the hall to his room, and when I got to the doorway, I saw he had dragged that neglected sewing machine out of the corner, opened it up, and had instruction books and bobbins and spools of thread all sitting out. "Hey Lynney," he said to me (Lynney was his affectionate name for me; no one else called me Lynney.) "Hey Lynney, how would you like it if you and I taught ourselves how to sew?"

HOME AWAY FROM HOME

LIVING WITH MAMA

I was visiting with my friend Terri when her husband, Denny, burst in the front door with a big smile on his face. "Lynne, I found the perfect RV for you."

RV? What does he mean, perfect RV? For me? Then I remembered a conversation we had recently.

Mama and I came to town almost every week to do shopping and errands, and to have Terri do Mama's hair and nails, the highlight of Mama's week. But the day was half gone by the time I got us out the door, what with packing extra clothes, meds, oxygen tanks, and wheelchair, and making the long drive. If Terri was available, I could leave Mama with her for the afternoon, but if not, that meant bringing Mama along to do errands, in and out of the car, in and out of the wheelchair, in and out of every store and shop.

One day I was grocery shopping, almost finished with my list, just one or two more things to get. Instead of pushing Mama's wheelchair with one hand (did you ever try to push a wheelchair with one hand?) and pulling the grocery cart behind me with the other, I had decided on the bright idea of leaving my grocery cart at the end of each aisle. Then I could push Mama in the wheelchair, put things in her lap as we went along, and then transfer them to the cart. I was feeling very self-satisfied as we wheeled down the last aisle, when I suddenly realized that my cart was gone. *I'm sure I left it right here... It's got to be here somewhere... I'm sure I parked it right around here... It's got to be here!* But it wasn't. Perhaps some customer decided they liked my choice of groceries better than their own and just went off with it. Maybe they thought it was their groceries. Or perhaps an overly zealous store employee decided it was an abandoned cart, abandoned for two minutes and, even as we stood there looking around, was efficiently replacing our groceries on all the appropriate shelves and bins.

As I was telling Terri and Denny my sad story that evening, Denny piped up with his idea. "You know Lynne, here's what you should do. You should get a little trailer or a little motorhome, and then your Mom could sit in there comfortably, with your dog Annie, and watch TV. And you could run in and out and get all your errands done in nothing flat."

I hadn't thought about the idea seriously, until Denny came in telling me about the perfect RV. Maybe it wasn't such a bad idea after all. I could just go look at it. Mama and I stayed in Terri and Denny's guest room that night, as we often did. Being the most gracious and generous hosts in the world, they always did everything to make us feel welcome, but I still felt uncomfortable imposing on them, over and over, week after week.

The next morning, I went out to the RV lot, and when I came back to Denny and Terri's, I was the one with the big smile on my face. "Yup!" I said to their questioning look, "I bought it." They were both happy for me, especially Denny because it was his idea.

It was old. Well, not extremely old, but fairly old. "It's a classic," I told myself as I looked at the faded and weathered exterior. No dents, no body damage. "That's good," I thought. It was a small, old-fashioned-style camper over an even smaller pickup truck. Four cylinders, underpowered and top-heavy. "Well, that's O.K.," I hoped. After all, it was a great deal.

It was the inside that sold me, an excellent floor plan, open and roomy, if you can call a tiny camper roomy, with large windows to let in lots of light. Those old-style windows weren't very burglar-proof, however. I locked myself out of the motor-home once, and just climbed in the window. That was before I had the sense to have a spare hide-a-key. The slightly worn upholstery of the sofa and dinette was in my favorite shades of light blue and soft tan, and the pretend wood cabinets were a warm shade of honey brown. "I can do something with this," I thought, "to make it even more personal," and I went to work on our new little home-away-from-home.

I gathered an assortment of comfy pillows, throws and afghans in complementary colors. Then I made up the dinette to be a permanent bed for Mama, with rubber sheets, flannel sheets, extra-soft padding, and a pretty coverlet. Beneath the dinette was the perfect storage area for the bulky oxygen tanks, which we had to take everywhere—stored out of sight, but handy. My bed was up above the truck cab, complete with feather pillows, down comforter, privacy curtain, and a reading light. Perfect. Amazingly, the old refrigerator still worked, and I stocked it with Mama's orange juice, which she loved, her meds, and special treats for lunches, snacks, and bedtime indulgences. The old venetian blinds over the kitchen and bathroom sinks went to the trash bin, and I replaced them with cream-colored window shades and lace curtains. I liked the tan draperies in the other areas, and dressed them up with brass rods and rings. The tan carpet was dingy so I shampooed it, which didn't help much, and covered it with brown braided rugs, a very down-home touch. On the tiny amount of wall space, I arranged personal decorations and mementoes, and hung a crystal in the kitchen to catch rainbows. Mama always loved stuffed animals, and we had them everywhere, tucked into almost every corner and propped up on every pillow. The cream-colored ceiling of the camper had become slightly stained around the skylights, probably from moisture seeping in over the years, and so I bought dozens of decorative stickers, everything from flowers and butterflies to cartoon characters, and covered the ceiling until there wasn't a stain in sight. I replaced the old toilet with a new, modern one when the old black-water tank fell out on the freeway. Yes! Actually fell out on the freeway!

We had air-conditioning for warm days and a forced-air furnace for chilly nights. And as for entertainment for Mama, I bought a little TV that had a built-in VCR player. This was in the days before DVDs, of course. I had an assortment of videos that I played for Mama while I ran in and out of stores. She didn't remember that she had seen the same video before, or if she did, she didn't care. She would sit with her feet propped up on a small footstool, her orange juice on a tray on one side of the sofa and Annie on her other side, close enough to pet. When I went into a store, I would set a kitchen timer for twenty minutes, and carry it around with me. When the timer went off, I would run out to the camper and peek in the window. More often than not, Mama was napping comfortably, the video playing, and Annie wagging at me through the window. Then I would run back in the store, hoping nobody had taken my cart in my absence. Denny was right. I got my errands done in nothing flat.

It turned out that the best thing about our camper was the amazingly reliable engine. It never, ever let us down or left us stranded. Like "The Little Engine That Could," it was slow going up our steep mountain roads, but it always brought us safely home. In mild weather, I would drive the camper back and forth from our home to the city, but when winter came, I would leave the RV in Denny and Terri's driveway, and make the commute in our trusty four-wheel-drive Jeep.

One cold afternoon, I was going through the last preparations for our trip back up the mountain, emptying the camper. I lugged out the heavy oxygen tanks and put them in the back of the Jeep, then brought out the groceries, clothes and packages and put them in the back seat. Mama had been sitting on the sofa in the camper, watching me work. When I was finally finished, I got our warm jackets and started to help Mama put on hers. She looked at me and said in a puzzled voice, "Honey, where are we going?"

I told her, "We're going home, Mama."

She looked around at our surroundings, the lace curtains, the colorful pillows and coverlets, the stuffed animals, and said with her sweet smile, "But honey, we're already home."

INTERNATIONAL CUISINE

The summer I was fifteen, I met a girl named Valerie. Her aunt and uncle, who were Swiss, lived on our street, and she had come over from Switzerland to visit them during her summer vacation. Since I had to stay home during the week to care for my five-year-old brother, Jimmy, it was so wonderful for me to have a new friend right in my own neighborhood. And Valerie was such a lovely girl: tall, blond, pretty, outgoing and confident. At that time, I was a shy teenager, young for my age, unsure of myself, and timid about trying anything new. Valerie was the perfect companion for me at that point in my life. A year older than I was, and a world traveler, she encouraged me in everything. We tried on each other's clothes, styled each other's hair, and traded makeup.

Valerie also helped me with one of my hobbies, a dollhouse made from an orange-crate. I had carved several small pieces of furniture from wood with a little help from my Daddy and his woodworking tools. The "faucets" on the sink and tub were ornate brass tacks and the sink was up on a little pedestal. I had decorated my dollhouse with terrycloth bath towels, homemade embroidered bedspreads, and a cradle holding a tiny pink baby doll. Valerie and I worked together on my dollhouse that summer. She made curtains, pillows and rugs in colors that I never would have imagined. My orange-crate cottage began to take on the look of a Swiss chalet!

On weekends, Valerie and I would ride our bikes several miles to the city pool. When I remember back to how over-protective my Mama was, I am amazed she allowed me to go, since I had never been to a swimming pool before and didn't know how to swim. But Valerie taught me, from the dead-man float to the butterfly stroke.

One Saturday when I was over at Valerie's house, she took a brick of Jack cheese from her aunt's refrigerator, cut a few slices, and offered me some. I had never even heard of Jack cheese, let alone tasted it. I loved it.

That evening I asked Mama if we could go to the grocery store and buy some Jack cheese. Evidently, she had never heard of it either, because she got a slightly disdainful look on her face, as if I had suggested we buy snails for escargot, and said, "Jack cheese? What is that?" I enthusiastically launched into my campaign speech, telling her how Valerie's aunt and uncle had that kind of cheese at their house, and Valerie had given me some, and it was really wonderful, and couldn't we buy it?

Mama looked at me sternly, shook her head and said, "No, Lynne, we are not going to buy that kind of cheese. We are Americans, and in this house, we eat American cheese."

I guess that was the reason we had fried chicken and apple pie every Sunday, because we were Americans. And I guess we had creamed tuna on toast every Friday, because we were Catholic. The closest we ever got to international cuisine was Van de Kamps cheese enchiladas. I'm not sure how the Dutch Van de Kamps and the Mexican enchiladas figured into the All-American theme, but it was a welcome change from meatloaf and hamburgers.

So, I appealed to my Daddy for help. After all, he wasn't Catholic, and his grandfather was French. Fortunately, his idea of patriotism didn't exclude trying new food. He and I went to the grocery store together and found Jack cheese in the delicatessen, right next to the American cheese. We brought it home, and ate it on our All-American Ritz crackers, with a dab of French's mustard. It was really delicious!

DON'T SPARE THE ROD

THE GOOD OLD DAYS

When I look back on my childhood, I remember many ways in which it was a very happy time. We always had all the necessities of life, and I felt safe, loved by my parents, and liked by many friends.

I was a very good little girl growing up, raised by a strict mother with high expectations, and taught by even stricter Catholic nuns in their intimidating black habits and ever-handy rulers for knuckle-rapping. I never broke the rules at school, and never disobeyed my parents, always trying to do what I was told to do.

• • • • •

In my youngest years Mama was always sweet and loving with me, but after I started school, things gradually began to change. One day, I came home from first grade in tears. Some of the other kids had laughed at me, telling me I was a baby because I still believed in Santa Claus. Instead of consoling me, Mama told me to stop crying and acting like a baby. I was a big girl now, and of course there was no Santa Claus. That didn't make sense to my six-year-old mind. But when I tried to tell her that she was the one who had told me about Santa, she got even more irritated with me and demanded I stop talking about it.

In second grade, I joined the Brownies. We had little brown dresses and neck scarves and worked to earn badges, just like the big Girl Scouts.

One Saturday we had a "cookout" in Mrs. Smith's backyard. She was our leader and lived in a huge mansion, complete with maids in black-and-white uniforms. We made "stoves" out of coffee cans, lit a brick of charcoal in the bottom, and fried strips of bacon on the top. It was an accident waiting to happen. Unfortunately, it happened to me: I burned my hand on the bacon grease.

Mrs. Smith took me into her kitchen and had her maid put baking soda and cool water in a bowl for me to soak my hand. When Mrs. Smith came back from phoning my Mama, the maid was leaning over me on the floor, saying very excitedly, "I don't know what happened, Ms. Smith; she just keeled over!" I had evidently fainted.

In the car on the way home, Mama was very angry with me. She accused me of pretending to faint, just to get attention. At seven years of age, I'm not sure I even knew what fainting was. In my entire life I had never told a lie to my Mama, or to anyone else for that matter. I was hurt and confused that she would think otherwise. But nothing I could say would convince her I was telling the truth.

When I was in the fourth grade, the girls in my class were all involved in collecting playing cards. I had the best collection of all. My parents played Bridge and Canasta and gave me the jokers from all their decks: pictures of animals, scenery and famous paintings, including my two new favorites, Pinky and Blue Boy.

At school one day we were eating lunch on the benches in the covered patio. We were not allowed to talk—don't ask me why. So, when my friend Katie wanted to see my new cards, without saying a single word, I quietly took out my cards and showed them to her. The nun saw this little exchange, came over, and took away my cards. I begged her not to take them, telling her that I had not been talking. But she just scowled at me, turned on her heel and marched off, shoving my beloved cards in her pocket.

That evening at home I pleaded with my Mama to go to school and get my cards back, telling her I had not said a word to Katie. She just said sharply that if I hadn't done something wrong, I wouldn't have gotten in trouble. The pain of losing my beautiful cards was not as bad as the grief of realizing my Mama didn't trust me or believe in me. (Now, years later, I look back on that incident, and wonder if my tough, feisty Mama was actually afraid to go to the school and confront that intimidating nun.)

• • • • •

One Christmas, my father's mother, my Grama Nini, gave me three antique dolls. I was enchanted with them but as soon as Nini left to go home, Mama took the dolls away from me and packed them in a box, telling me I wasn't old enough and responsible enough to take care of them. She never even allowed me to look at them when she was home. I never saw those dolls again until after I was married. I went over to my parents' house when my Mama wasn't home and took the dolls home with me. But they brought back only sad memories, so I ended up giving them to the Goodwill. I regret that now; I would love to have Nini's dolls today. I can only hope they found a good home.

On another Christmas, I received a corduroy dress, bright orange, with a shoulder-wide collar and a zipper right down the front. When I told Mama I didn't like the dress, she told me that was because I hadn't any sense of style. Mama was the most stylish lady I knew, and so for years I didn't think I had any style. Eventually, I realized I have my own look of what works for me. And hey, even today when I remember that dress, I think it was hideous!

And on yet another Christmas, my parents bought me a used piano. It was waiting there for me on Christmas morning with a big red bow fastened on it. But that gift quickly turned into a source of grief for me. I took piano lessons at school from a nun who smacked my fingers with a ruler when I made a mistake. And I practiced at home with a mother who made me play an extra half hour if she caught me looking at my hands instead of at the music. I remember her saying, "You're not reading the music, you're memorizing it." And it was never the kind of music I wanted to play, like the tunes my friends learned, but only the classics that the nuns thought appropriate. After a few years of struggling through lessons and practicing, never to Mama's satisfaction, I came home from school one day to find my piano gone. Mama had sold it without a word of warning, without my even knowing about it. When I tried to ask her about it, she just told me she was tired of telling me to practice, and that was the end of it. (But that wasn't the end of it. I'm amazed that I grew up to be a musician, and that I've spent most of my adult life teaching and sharing my love of music with others.)

• • • • •

Then a series of events happened that, in retrospect, combined together to be the worst setback of my young life. It started on the first day of Easter vacation. I was riding my bike around the block. Although I was twelve years old, I wasn't allowed to ride in the street or the alley. At the end of the block a group of neighbor kids were playing jump rope in the alley driveway. When they saw me coming on my bike, they started calling to me to ride through the rope. They swung it as high as they could and I ducked down, trying to get under the arch. But I not only didn't make it through, the rope pulled me off my bike, and as I fell, the bike pedal broke my leg. To punish me for playing in the alley, Mama would not allow the doctor to give me a walking cast or crutches. Instead, I had to stay in bed for three months, no baths or showers, no shampoos, and worst of all a bedpan. A few days later, lying in bed, lonely and in pain, I sassed Mama about something, and she took my Easter basket full of candy and threw it in the trash.

Then that summer, our family moved to a new house, to my Mama's and Daddy's delight and my dismay. I had no visitors all summer, and didn't even have a chance to say goodbye to my friends. In September when I started at my new school, I had a terrible limp from my still painful broken leg. For some reason that I do not understand to this day, Mama forbad me to tell my new classmates that I had broken my leg the previous summer. I was such an obedient child that I did not disobey her.

Then, two weeks after school started, the students were given an eye exam, something I never had before. My test showed amblyopia, "lazy eye," and I had to wear a black eye patch and horrible tortoiseshell horn-rimmed glasses. My long, pretty hair was cut very short from my summer in bed; we had to wear ugly uniforms at the new school; and on top of it all, I started getting acne. I was the only new kid in class and what a freak I was: limping, black eye patch, ugly glasses, hacked-off hair, acne, lonely, sad, and unaccepted.

When Mama went to work full time, I had to stay home to baby-sit my little brother after school and during summer vacation. I was unable to attend after-school activities or visit at classmates' homes. It took me years to develop friendships at my new school and decades to grow past my sense of not belonging.

One summer, my lonely days at home were brightened by a new little pet. I already had my little dog Inky, a black curly fellow who loved only me. Although he wasn't allowed in the house, he was my dear companion and we spent happy times together. Then some friends of our family who raised birds gave us a little parakeet, a darling little thing, light blue in color and very friendly. Mama was not happy about the present because birds are messy, and she was a very fastidious housekeeper. She said we could keep it as long as I kept it in its cage.

When I was home alone, babysitting for my little brother, I would open the cage door, and put my hand in to pet and play with the little bird. One day it slipped out past my arm and flew across the room, landing on a shelf. I immediately rushed over, picked it up and put it back in its cage. But when Mama discovered a bird dropping on the shelf, she knew I had disobeyed her, and so she got rid of the bird. She was so angry at me that she wanted to also get rid of my little dog, Inky, to punish me. But Daddy talked her out of that, saying Inky was so attached to me that he would be miserable in another home.

• • • • •

Sometimes things would happen that would cause Mama to show her gentle, affectionate side to me, reassuring me that she really did love me and appreciate me. In preparation for Christmas one year, I walked down to the five-and-dime store, and bought a set of pillowcases for Mama and Daddy. They were part of an embroidery kit. The material was stamped with a pattern in ink, and a selection of colorful embroidery threads was included to complete the project. Remembering back, they were probably rather gaudy and certainly corny, but not to my adolescent eyes. The drawings were of two "southern belles" in overlapping hoop skirts with the ruffle on the edge of the pillowcase being the skirt "hem." The body of the gowns was decorated with flowers and garlands, the colors and stitches to be determined by the seamstress. How I loved those beautiful dresses, visions of "Gone with the Wind" floating through my imagination. Fortunately, I had purchased my gifts early, because it took me weeks and weeks to complete them. And being a beginner at needlework, I had to take out and redo sections here and there.

I worked on my sewing in my bedroom, sitting on the floor on the far side of the bed, partly out of sight from the doorway. When I heard someone coming down the hall, I would shove my materials under the bed, pick up my book and pretend to be reading. It was usually Mama, wanting to know what I was doing wasting my time reading; why didn't I have my chores done, and insisting I come into the kitchen right now.

Christmas morning finally came, and I was much more excited about giving Mama and Daddy my gift than I was about what presents I would receive. Mama opened my package, and then just sat there with my embroidery in her lap for the longest time. Finally, she looked up and said, "When I think of all the times I scolded you for sitting in your room reading, and these beautiful pillowcases were what you were making." Then she started crying, tears just running down her face. She hugged me and told me they were the loveliest embroidery she had ever seen. And I guess they were because she used those pillowcases on their bed until they just literally fell apart.

• • • • •

As an adult, I now look back on such events and try to understand Mama's thinking. I believe that, to her, the world was a hard place. Taking care of a family, trying to have a decent life was a constant struggle. I remember her showing me a scar on her knee, and telling me a story about when she was a little girl. Her father was going to spank her, so she ran out the door and down the road. She stumbled and fell in the gravel, cutting her knee so deeply that she still had the scar forty years later. Her father caught up with her, lying in the road, crying and bleeding, and spanked her right there. She was hit or spanked often, even into her young adult years.

However, thinking back yet another generation, my Grampa Dannemiller (her father), through hard work and ingenuity, had kept his family from being homeless or starving during the Depression. This was a man who was raised to believe that a husband was the head of his home, to be obeyed without question by his wife and children. This was the era of "spare the rod, spoil the child" mentality. To him, and to many others in that time, the world was indeed a hard place, and harsh discipline for himself and his family was necessary to survive.

We are what we live, and Mama's life and attitudes about raising children were shaped by a domineering father.

• • • • •

[Daddy]

My own father, however, was a gentle and generous husband and parent. Although he worked long hours, from very early in the morning until late in the day, he often took time to do special things for all of us.

Our new home, where we moved when I was twelve, was a three-bedroom house on a quiet street in West Los Angeles. It was a nice, attractive neighborhood, where kids played four-square ball in the street and hopscotch on the sidewalks. But the house was really beat up: holes in the walls, damaged floors, broken windows. Daddy patched and painted and sanded and varnished. He mowed and weeded and planted rosebushes for Mama.

When I was away for a weekend, to surprise me, my parents decorated my room—pink of course! They furnished it with used furniture that Daddy painted a soft creamy white: a beautiful wooden headboard with raised flowers and garlands, a chest-on-chest, and a little vanity top with a white cotton skirt trimmed with eyelet lace and pink ribbon. I even had a tiny pink lamp. Later Daddy built me corner bookshelves under the windows for my beloved books and even built me a desk. When my desktop radio was knocked to the floor and the plastic case was broken, Daddy built a radio case to match my desk.

On summer weekends, Daddy and I would work together out in the garage, he with his woodworking tools making custom rifle stocks, or things for the house, while I worked on my orange-crate dollhouse. All my furniture was made of wood, with a little help from Daddy.

My friend Valerie came over one day with a gift for my dollhouse, a tiny dresser with two moveable drawers, painted brown and made of cardboard. I thanked her graciously, but after she left, I told Daddy that I didn't want cardboard furniture. I wanted every piece to be carved out of wood. But Daddy gently reminded me that wasn't what was important. What did matter was the love behind the gift.

When I grew up and cared for my six children, I tried to remember Daddy's example, that what matters is the love you give. Of course, I made mistakes; every parent does, no matter how well-meaning we are. But I don't think I made the same mistakes that my Mama did. I never spanked my kids. I expected them to be polite and respectful, and I was always respectful of them. And I believed in them, that they were each precious and good and infinitely loveable. I tried to be kind and patient with them, as my Daddy always was with me.

The ironic thing is, years later when Mama came down with heart trouble and dementia, and lived with me for her last five years, she became this really sweet, funny, lovely little lady! Well, most of the time anyway. It seems this was who she really was, underneath that protective armor.

Mama and I were finally able to come full circle, each of us to give and to receive the gifts we had to share, the most important of all, the unconditional gift of love.

HOME FOR CHRISTMAS

"Oh goody!" Mama said, "We're going Christmas shopping!" I had to laugh with her. She was so excited. We were going down to the city to buy presents for the family and stay with our friends Terri and Denny. It was quite a project, getting us out the door, helping Mama bathe and dress, giving her her meds and inhalation therapy, and packing everything we needed for an overnight stay.

But we got ready in record time and managed to get a few errands done in town in the afternoon. It was slow-going because it meant taking the wheelchair and oxygen tank in and out of the car for every stop. But it was fun, being in the hustle bustle of holiday shoppers and seeing all the stores decorated for the season. We went out to eat with Terri and Denny, and then went back to their house where we had our little RV parked. We really had a nice day and as I got Mama settled down for the night, she and I talked about our shopping plans for the next day.

But during the night, I heard Mama coughing off and on, and by morning the cough was very persistent. Terri noticed Mama's cough too and suggested we go to a local hospital close by her house, just to get Mama checked out. It was a short drive there, but a long wait in the waiting room. I guess that's why they call them waiting rooms. Then followed a longer wait in the examination room, as first nurses and then doctors went through their procedures that were oh-so-familiar to Mama and me by now. Finally, they took an X-ray that showed a slight shadow at the bottom of one lung, maybe a little fluid they thought, probably nothing to be worried about since she had no other symptoms. I could take her back home with me that day and have our regular doctor check her out tomorrow, or I could leave her there for observation and pick her up tomorrow.

When I think back to that choice offered to me that morning, I'm ashamed when I remember my reaction. I immediately thought, "Oh boy, I can leave Mama here all day and run around and get all kinds of shopping done." Little did I know what awaited me. When I went back to visit her that evening, I learned she had stopped breathing and had slipped into a coma. My guilt about wanting to shop without being encumbered by her care was offset by the terrifying realization that if I had taken her home that day, she would have stopped breathing there, and surely would have died that night. It was only because she was on a monitor in the hospital that they were alerted immediately and put her on a ventilator. And there she remained... for three weeks! When she finally regained consciousness and was able to breathe on her own, the doctor told me that he considered it a miracle that she had survived.

Well, it was the season of miracles. Mama was back home for Christmas with me that year, and for several more years after that. Some of my kids and grandkids came to share dinner with us that day too, which made it even more special. And to top it all off, we even had a little snow! It was the perfect "White Christmas."

OUR LITTLE MASCOT

LIVING WITH MAMA

Oh, how Mama loved our music! She would clap her hands like a little child after each tune, whether it was an evening guitar class in our living room or a band performance somewhere in town.

When I first moved to the mountain, the only neighbors I knew were my long-time friends, Ron and Barbara. Ron took me under his musical wing and invited me to local music parties, sessions and band rehearsals. He asked me to join their band, "Rose of Tejon" which I agreed to do with the understanding that I might miss a rehearsal or even a performance, depending on Mama's health.

However, as the months went by and her health gradually improved—with excellent medical care from our local doctor, oxygen therapy, good nutrition and social interaction—she was often able to come with me to music events.

There followed several years of happy times and wonderful memories. At band rehearsals, Mama would sit, listening and smiling, petting our family dog, Annie. During sessions in the warm weather, Mama would be with us in her wheelchair as we gathered in the shade of an old oak tree, enjoying the music, the friends and the delicious food from the potluck. At winter sessions we all crowded together around the fire in the old antique store, where Mama had lots of company visiting with the other non-musicians in the kitchen.

For years we performed at the Annual Lilac Festival, playing our Celtic and old-timey tunes and selling our CDs. Mama was right there with us, tucked in the shade of the trees, where she sat sipping from her water bottle and wearing her tie-dyed dress. (I still have that dress today and wear it sometimes myself. It makes me smile.)

At the Contra Dances in the big dance hall where we played once a month, Mama sat right up front with us, smiling proudly at being one of the band. That's where she got her nickname. A handsome grey-haired gentleman came up to Mama during an intermission, took her hand and said, "And who are you, young lady?"

Mama smiled shyly and replied, "My name is Ann, and I'm here with my daughter and these nice folks."

"And are you a regular member of the group?" he asked kindly.

"Well yes, I guess I am," Mama said, sitting up a little straighter and smiling a little brighter. "I'm the... I'm their..." Suddenly she looked confused and looked over at us, questioningly. Michele, our fiddle player spoke right up. "Yes, she is. Ann is our most important member. We couldn't get along without her. She's our little mascot."

SALT AND PEPPER

I have a beautiful set of silver salt and pepper shakers, given to me by my Mama for my wedding shower. Actually, it is a salt shaker and pepper grinder, the grinder having a small, cleverly designed top that you twist to grind the peppercorns. I use the set frequently, especially when we have company, and often a dinner guest will look appreciatively at the pepper grinder, admiring its clever style and attractive appearance.

It makes me smile when I remember the circumstances of receiving this gift. In those days, it was often a custom to give a "theme" shower for the bride. It could be a "garden" theme for a girl who loved flowers and gardening, a "house" theme for a new bride-to-be who was into decorating, or a "kitchen" theme, for someone like me who liked to cook and bake.

My friend Jeannie, who had introduced me to my soon-to-be husband, gave me a "kitchen" shower. On each invitation, she wrote requests for each guest, asking them to tie a specific small kitchen accessory to the outside of their gift package, like a paring knife, a potato peeler, a spatula, a pot scrubber, and on Mama's invitation, a set of salt and pepper shakers. However, Mama misunderstood the instruction. She thought everyone was going to bring salt and pepper shakers, which were popular collector's items in those days, and since she was the mother of the bride, she decided that her salt and pepper shakers had to be the best! And, believe me, they were!

That shower started a new era in my relationship with my mother. She had always been very strict with me, sometimes overly so, and she was not the kind of Mom who hugs or kisses her kids. But I always knew my mother loved me very much, and after I married and was not her responsibility anymore, I think she saw me in a different light.

Mama, who kept an immaculate home, was very complimentary about how I decorated and cared for my own home, even when I had several little babies running about. When she and Daddy would come for dinner, at one of our numerous birthday or holiday celebrations, she would praise my cooking and ask me for recipes. She adored her grandchildren and, I noticed, she had no reservations about hugging and kissing them. She bought them beautiful clothes and toys, and often bought lovely things for me and for our home, as well. She even started giving me a little shy hug now and then.

As time went by, our relationship evolved into a warm and loving friendship between equals. We admired and respected each other, encouraged each other in our work and our dreams, and confided our worries, problems and challenges of life.

We became, truly, friends.

BLACK AND WHITE

"I'm glad I wasn't born black." Mama made this announcement after she and I had been watching a TV program that dealt with racial discrimination. I wasn't sure Mama even understood the program, but sometimes her insights amazed me so I asked her why she thought that and she said, "Well, because if you're black, people don't treat you well, even if you're a good person. But if you're white, people treat you better, even if you're a bad person."

Well, that was a simplified version of the plot of the show we had just watched. Mama had understood it better than I expected. "But, Mama, not all people think that way. Many people try to see a person as an individual, not just what color they are."

Mama seemed lost in thought for a few minutes. I thought she had forgotten about the matter. Then she said quietly, "Like Lucetta. I loved Lucetta. She was my friend."

Yes, she was. I hadn't thought about Lucetta for years. After I married and wasn't there to help Mama with the housework, Mama hired Lucetta to come in one day a week and do the "heavy cleaning." After many years of hard work, Mama and Daddy's financial position was much improved. Daddy was promoted from mail carrier to supervisor of the Olympic Station post office in Beverly Hills, and Mama was office manager of a prestigious real estate firm in the high-rent district of Westwood. She enjoyed the luxury of returning to her already immaculate and orderly home to find all the nooks and crannies freshly shined and polished. Lucetta did a fabulous job of exceeding Mama's high standards of home care, and their mutual respect grew into a long-standing friendship that lasted for more than thirty years.

I remembered one conversation Mama told me about that she had with Lucetta. Mama asked her if she ever got tired of cleaning houses and Lucetta told her, "Oh no, I very much enjoy cleaning houses. I have five clients, one for each weekday and I know exactly what I have to do at each home. It's quiet work and very satisfying. My sister, now she's a schoolteacher and you couldn't pay me enough money to deal with all those noisy kids, running around hollering all day!" She and Mama had a good laugh about that. I suspect Mama agreed with her!

Mama broke into my thoughts with her next opinion. "I don't see why God couldn't just make everybody the same color. Why didn't he do that?"

Thinking to myself that it wouldn't solve the problem of human conflict, I said, "Well maybe God just likes variety, Mama." Then in an effort to lighten up the subject with a bit of humor, I added, "See our little dog, Annie. She's black and other dogs, who might be white or brown or blond, don't treat her any differently."

Mama gave me such a look! I didn't know what she thought of my pathetic attempt at a joke, but she just shook her head seriously, and said, "That's because most dogs are nicer than most people."

SILVER CUPS

LIVING WITH MAMA

When my children were babies, it was the custom to give silver baby cups as gifts, engraved with the newborn's name and birthdate. Since Mama and Daddy were the godparents for all of our six children, Mama was the one who gave us the cups, each one a little different from the others, all of them lovely. Those cups were dropped by our babies on the kitchen floor hundreds of times, never breaking of course (that was the advantage of having silver instead of ceramic), but they eventually were covered with dents to the point where they wouldn't even sit up straight on the baby's highchair tray.

As time went by, I graduated the cups from the kitchen to the bathroom. I bought a folding wooden cup rack. Do you know the kind? With crisscrossed pieces of wood and a wooden peg at each intersection? I hung the rack up by the bathroom sink and put a cup on each peg for the children to use after brushing their teeth—much more charming than the mini-paper-cup dispensers that were popular back then.

After my children were grown and out on their own, I found other ways to display those little cups. The least-dented cup, belonging to my oldest daughter Cindy, found a place of honor in my display cabinet in my living room, along with a silver baby spoon and fork, and next to an antique china baby dish that originally belonged to my Grampa. That dish was used by my Uncle Bill, my Mama, me, my brother, and all six of my children. When my young baby dropped the dish on the kitchen floor one day, I picked it up, looked at the sweet picture of rosy-cheeked children clustered around a bowl of fruit, a picture that was faded by the thousands of times a baby's chubby little hand had dragged a silver baby spoon across the surface of the plate, and thought, "Good heavens! This dish is irreplaceable!" I put it in my display cabinet to be safely admired but not used. I hung the other cups on a wooden peg rack, along with other kitchen utensils on my kitchen wall.

But when Mama lived with me, my favorite use for those silver cups was to fill one with cookies and keep it on the side table next to her chair. Mama loved that little cup. I doubt if she remembered she had given it to me decades ago, but hardly a day went by that she didn't hold it up admiringly and say, "Isn't this the prettiest little cup?" And for all its dings and dents, it still was. Those silver cups had come full circle.

One evening she said to me, "Honey, will you put some cookies in my little cup?"

"In a little while, Mama," I answered. "I'm going to give you some dinner first." It was the old "dinner before dessert" rule that she used to say to me when I was a kid, only now I was saying it to her. Not that she remembered; she didn't. But this time she had a different reason for asking.

"Well, yes, but I like to keep some cookies in this little cup. In case someone comes over to visit me, I'll have some cookies to offer them."

I loved it when she came up with stuff like that! I knew that our little dog Annie was the only one who ever got to beg one of those cookies from Mama. But then, somehow, it didn't matter.

"Oh, I see. I didn't know about that." I'm sure I had a big grin on my face when I went to get the cookies.

What the heck. Life is short. Eat dessert first.

[A family gathering]

TOMMY'S CARD TRICK

At a family gathering many years ago, my oldest son Tom, or Tommy as we called him then, brought his deck of cards over to Mama and said, "Grama, I want to show you a card trick!" He was about seven years old at the time and very proud of the fact that he had mastered a trick that impressed even the grown-ups.

My beautiful mother didn't fit the stereotype of the average grandmother except, like most grandparents, she adored her grandchildren and enjoyed the attention from her "number one grandson," as she affectionately called Tommy.

They sat down together and Tommy shuffled his cards. Then he carefully fanned them out face-down and held them out in front of himself. With a big grin he said, "Pick a card, Grama, any card!"

At first glance, the back of the cards appeared to be a symmetrical scroll pattern, but if you looked closely, "right-side up" was slightly different from "upside down." This, of course, was the key to the trick.

As my mother took one of the cards and looked at it, Tommy closed the deck and discreetly rotated it in the opposite direction. Then he said, "O.K. Grama, you put your card back without showing it to me, and then I'll mix up the cards and then I'll tell you which one is yours." He fanned the cards out one more time and offered them to my mother. She started to replace her card in the deck when she noticed that its scroll pattern was opposite from the other cards so she meticulously rotated her card and slipped it back in place! Tommy sat there for several seconds with a bewildered look on his face and then he blurted out, "Grama, you ruined my card trick!"

For years after that, we teased Mama about being so neat that she couldn't even put a card in the deck "up side down!"

ANNIE, THE HERO DOG

LIVING WITH MAMA

When we think of heroic dogs, we imagine St. Bernards with kegs of brandy rescuing skiers trapped by avalanches, or Border Collies protecting their sheep herd from ravenous packs of wolves! Somehow, a little twelve-pound curly black poodle doesn't fit that image. But there are all kinds of heroes. Quiet, unpretentious, day-in-and-day-out heroes, just being there for those they love, no matter what it takes.

When I first got Annie as a young puppy, she was a one-man dog, or in my case, a one-woman dog! Although she loved people and craved affection from all my visitors, I was the one person she wanted to be with at all times. If I went upstairs, she raced up with me. Whatever room I was in, she had to be in the same room with me. If I left the house without her, she cowered down on the floor, crumpled and pathetic. Then she would watch for me at the window until I returned, no matter what hour of the day or night.

But when Mama came to live with me, Annie decided it was her job to be the full-time caretaker. One of my most cherished pictures is of Mama, wearing her favorite blue robe, her slight frame looking almost childlike as she sat in a big overstuffed chair with little Annie cuddled on the seat next to her.

Because of poor circulation, Mama usually felt cold despite warm clothing and fleece-lined boots. Even the comforting heat radiating from the pellet stove next to her rocker, and cozy afghans wrapped around her feet and legs propped up on the ottoman, weren't enough. But when Annie stretched her warm, curly self across Mama's legs, she finally felt comfortable and comforted.

At night I tucked Mama in bed, snuggled in a warm flannel nightie, socks, and blankets, that I had just pulled out of the hot clothes dryer. Then Annie would hop up to her self-appointed post at the foot of the bed and put her chin on Mama's feet. Even though I was busy in other rooms, Annie wouldn't come to be with me until I went to bed myself, and then she would come upstairs to sleep on my bed.

One night, sometime in the wee hours, I was awakened out of a sound sleep by Annie jumping on me, barking and running up and down the stairs. I finally woke up enough to realize something was wrong. Downstairs, on the floor beside her bed, Mama lay crumpled in a little heap. Although I was programmed to waken when she called me, much like a mother hears her newborn infant waken for a middle-of-the-night feeding, I hadn't been able to hear her quiet whimpering, but Annie heard her. She had fallen on the way to or from the bathroom. When I tried to lift her up, she cried out in pain. She had a dinner plate sized bruise on her ribs where she had fallen, evidently from hitting the edge of a heavy magazine rack.

Later X-rays showed, amazingly, no broken bones, although she was bedridden for several days because she was in so much pain. I hate to think how long she could have been there on the floor that night, too injured to move and too disoriented to call for help. If it hadn't been for Annie, little hero dog Annie, I probably wouldn't have found her until morning.

From that point on, Annie would "check up" on Mama during the night. I would be dimly aware of her coming up the stairs to my room, jumping back on the bed, turning around in circles and then settling back down to sleep. And sometimes in the morning when I awoke, I would find Annie, not in my bed, but downstairs in Mama's bed, and not at the foot of the bed either, but curled up in Mama's arms.

YOU'RE SO PRETTY

Mama saw the beauty in her surroundings. I kept flowers on her side table, just a tiny bouquet from the grocery store, but she would lean over to smell them several times a day. When I brought her orange juice, she would admire the glass. It was a pretty glass - it belonged to my Grama - cranberry glass, they called it. But the point was Mama noticed it. When I dressed her in a velour blouse on a cool day, she would run her hand down the soft sleeve and say, "Oh, this feels so nice!" She wore her pearl bracelet and gold watch every day, and I would often notice her looking at them, straightening them on her wrist, admiring them.

Mama saw beauty in people too. Whenever we had guests or went out with friends, Mama would always find something complimentary to say: "You have such lovely hair," or "That's a pretty outfit you're wearing," or to the gentlemen, "You, sir, are very handsome!"

Because I was around her the most, I was on the receiving end of regular compliments. I would come downstairs in the morning and no matter whether I was wearing a nice dress or just work clothes, Mama would usually say, "You look so pretty this morning, honey." It always made me feel good.

We had a little joke between us. When I told her she looked pretty, she would say, "I must have caught it from you." When she told me I looked pretty, I would say, "I must have inherited it from my Mama." And then we would both laugh. I don't think she always understood that she was my mother, but she laughed as though she did.

One day I was driving our Jeep down to the city. Mama leaned over from the passenger seat, put her hand on my arm, and said, "You look so pretty today, honey." Concentrating on the heavy traffic, I didn't answer her right away. She gave me a little pat and said sweetly, "Now you can say, 'I must have inherited it from my Mama.'"

[Lynne & Mama]

SPOONS

"O.K. kids! Everybody ready?" My young children were standing around the kitchen table, grinning and giggling.

I was at my kitchen sink, which was filled with hot soapy water, and as I called, "Spoons!" each child grabbed a spoon, ran over to the sink and dropped their spoon into the water. As I started washing quickly, I called "Forks!" Within seconds all the forks were in the hot water. The game continued with me calling for another item on the table, never in the same order, and all the children grabbing them as fast as they could and bringing them for me to wash. In a few short minutes the entire table was empty and I was almost finished washing. The plates were in the drainer rack, the serving dishes were covered and in the refrigerator, and the napkins, homemade from sturdy brown material, were in the clothes hamper. Then I would call out, "Ready, set, go!" And all the children would run out of the kitchen full speed.

Each night, however, one child was excused from the kitchen, if they would go into the nearby den and play the piano for us. My daughter, Cindy, always played her tunes so nicely, but sometimes when one of the boys was "entertaining" us, the cacophony coming from the piano wasn't very musical!

The kitchen in the house where we raised our big family was my favorite room; large, bright and sunny, with an oval maple table and eight chairs all around. I usually had flowers from our garden in a white milk-glass flower bowl as a centerpiece. The table settings were old-fashioned but charming. The glasses that we had back then, in the days before plastic, were white hobnail milk glass, the bumpy exterior making them quite slip-proof. The plates and bowls were brown and white pottery with "old pioneer" scenes on them. I had accumulated those dishes week by week from our local supermarket: "Spend $20 on groceries and earn a free plate, bowl, or serving dish." All quite utilitarian.

Except for our silverware. It was real sterling silver, and I used it every day, which appalled my Mama who thought I should "save it for good." I received two settings of silver as a wedding gift from my parents and then another knife, fork or spoon for each birthday and Christmas after that. I knew I should be using it just for holiday meals, but I loved the look of it and the feel of it in my hand. With a large family of young children, I didn't have many indulgent luxuries but this was one of them. And besides, I rationalized, if you use your silver every day you hardly ever have to polish it. We never lost, bent, or damaged a single piece and I use and enjoy that silver to this day.

One summer, my Mama's parents, Grama and Grampa Dannemiller, came from Ohio to California for a visit. I was very nervous at the thought of entertaining them. My Grampa was a hard-working and successful man who owned his own business. He was a man of few words, used to giving orders and expecting everything to be his way. When I was a kid, he was always short and gruff with me and I always felt he disapproved of me. My Grama, however, was the sweetest, dearest lady you could ever want for a Grama. But since she was an immaculate housekeeper and a wonderful cook, I was sure I couldn't live up to their expectations. However, I was determined to try.

I cleaned my house (well, the front part of it, anyway) the morning of their visit, and prepared my favorite recipes with the greatest care. The table was set with our best dishes and a centerpiece of roses from our garden. Our children had clean clothes, polished shoes, clean fingernails, and combed hair. I reminded them about table manners and "please" and "thank you." As for myself, I wore one of my favorite dresses, a dress I never wore for cooking, but this was a very special occasion. My husband looked very nice and was the perfect host. He was the only one I didn't have to worry about!

Well, the evening went wonderfully. We were a bit crowded, but we managed quite well. All the food looked and tasted better than I could have hoped. The children looked darling (I'm blessed with cute kids), and behaved beautifully. Mama gave me many approving smiles and nods as the evening progressed. My Grama complimented me on everything as was her sweet way. And even my Grampa let down his usual gruff exterior, said the meal was delicious, and told my husband and me that he admired our well-behaved children.

But then, when the meal was over, pandemonium broke out. The kids jumped up from their chairs, shoved and banged the chairs back against the table, accidentally bumping into the startled guests who were trying to rise from the table also. They started giggling and jostling for their position in the circle, and waited for the games to begin.

I stood speechless and frozen for several seconds. My careful facade of a quiet, polite, orderly home and family had just evaporated into thin air. What now? I walked over to the sink, turned on the hot water, and yelled, "Spoons!"

Fortunately, my Grampa saw the humor in the whole situation. Maybe he remembered being a kid once himself, about a hundred years ago. Anyway, as he was leaving that night, he came up to me, told me again how much he had enjoyed the dinner, and, with a twinkle in his eye, said he also enjoyed meeting our children. Then he handed me a check for $300.

"Buy a dishwasher," he said. He wanted me to have something to make my life a little easier. And he said he wanted to give it to me now, when I could really use it, and while he was still alive to know I was enjoying it.

Gosh, I guess Grampa really did approve of me after all.

UNCLE BILL'S VISIT

LIVING WITH MAMA

Mama and I looked forward to her brother Bill's visit the way children look forward to Christmas. We talked about it for weeks ahead of time, looked at Uncle Bill and Aunt Celia's picture that Mama kept beside her chair, and reminisced about her childhood in rural Ohio.

Mama remembered the Great Depression and how her family ate cornmeal mush day in and day out. Her enterprising father packaged dried corn for popping in little brown paper bags and sold them door-to-door to his neighbors, the modest beginning of the C. J. Dannemiller Company. Bill worked for the company all his life and now my cousins and many of my nephews and nieces work in the family business also, which has expanded greatly since the 1930s and flourishes to this day. It's an All-American success story!

I also heard many stories (over and over!) about Bill when he was young, how he was so handsome and kind, and the scholar of the family. Bill got all "A's" on his report cards, but Mama got "B's" in arithmetic! Bill was also an outstanding athlete, captain of the football team.

My Aunt Celia had recently told me that, although Uncle Bill was now well into his 80s and retired, he still went down to the warehouse regularly to "help out." He even mowed the lawn out front with a push mower and pruned the bushes with hand shears!

We counted the days until Uncle Bill would fly to California with my cousin Jim. When the day finally arrived, it was a touching sight to see the two of them, Bill and my Mama, finally together after many years separation.

Bill came in the door with his son Jim, and Mama got up slowly from her chair, took off her oxygen, carefully straightened her favorite blue robe, and then walked unsteadily across the room. As Bill came forward to greet her, holding out both his hands, he started to shake her hand, and then they just fell into each other's arms, hugging and kissing and laughing. Jim and I looked at each other over their heads, both of us thinking the same thing; this would be their last visit together.

My cousin Jim had accompanied his dad from Ohio to California. He knew that Bill was too forgetful to make the trip alone. Uncle Bill agreed, telling us that his doctor had prescribed... what is the name of that medicine?"

"Ginkgo Biloba," Jim reminded him.

"Oh yes, Ginkgo Bil... Ginkgo something. Well anyway, I take it twice a day, if I can remember!"

Like many older people, Mama and Bill had little trouble remembering the old days. They reminisced for hours, through the afternoon and into the evening, talking about friends, family, and days gone by.

During the visit, Mama, the gracious hostess, turned to my cousin Jim, to include him in the conversation, and asked, "And what is your name, young man?"

Jim, the "young man" who was in his 60s at the time, answered ever so kindly, "My name's Jim. I'm your brother Bill's oldest son."

And Mama said, "Oh, that's a nice name. I have a son named Jim. He's just about your age." (She was referring to my brother Jim who had died several years before, but fortunately she didn't remember that. She also didn't realize that of course Jim knew his own cousin.)

A few minutes later Mama looked over at Jim and said, "And what's your name, young man?" and he answered again, "My name's Jim. I'm your brother's son." And then Mama said again, "Oh, that's a nice name. I have a son. His name is Jim also." This little scene played itself out over and over throughout the visit, with Jim, the perfect gentleman, answering patiently, with never a change from his pleasant smile or his affectionate tone of voice to betray the fact that he had now gone through this exchange several times.

Jim and Bill were still on Eastern Standard Time and jet lag was catching up with them both, so they decided to go to bed early. They had barely disappeared up the stairs when Mama waved me over and asked in a conspiratorial whisper, "Who was that man sitting over there in that chair?"

Of course I thought she was still asking about Jim, but then I realized she was pointing to the chair where her brother had been sitting. "Mama, that's your brother Bill!"

"No, it's not," she replied with a look on her face like she knew I was kidding her.

"Yes, it is!" (What else could I say?)

"But he doesn't look like his picture," she said, picking up the frame from beside her chair and showing it to me.

"Well, that's a pretty old picture, Mama. I guess Bill does look older now, but then we all look older now, don't we?" I tease her, trying to make her feel better about not recognizing Bill.

With a little frown, she asked, "Well, did I talk to him like he was my brother?"

I reached out to her and gave her a hug. "Of course, Mama, you had a very nice visit with him."

"Well, thank goodness," she murmured, giving me a wry little smile. "I wouldn't want to make a fool of myself!"

MY BIRTHSTONE RING

For my thirtieth birthday, my Mama gave me a beautiful topaz and diamond ring. At the time, I had a houseful of young children and lived on a modest income, so a piece of fine jewelry was especially cherished.

And it was so lovely: three emerald-cut stones of golden topaz (my birthstone), set diagonally in 14-carat gold, with two small diamonds tucked above and two below. I treasured it dearly and wore it every day.

Some years later, my friend Mary and I went for an outing to Knott's Berry Farm. After spending a wonderful day shopping and sightseeing, we left and went to a restaurant for dinner. Sitting there at the table, reading the menu, I looked down at my hand and saw that my ring was gone! I realized immediately what I had done. Earlier in the day, as we had driven into the parking lot of Knott's, I had taken off my ring, laid it on the lap of my skirt to put on hand lotion, and then had gotten out of the car, forgetting my ring!

We rushed out of the restaurant to the car, hoping to find the ring on the car floor, but it wasn't there. As Mary drove back to Knott's, I was sick at heart. How could I have been so careless with my precious ring?

As we pulled into the parking lot, my mood sank from heartsick to hopeless. The lot was a huge area of mowed crabgrass, with a few stubby palm trees here and there. It was absolutely impossible to tell where we had parked earlier. We stopped, got out, and started wandering around, although it seemed a complete waste of time. Someone could have seen the ring and picked it up, or a car could have driven over it. More likely, it had just settled down into the grass, out of sight, probably far away from where we were looking. And it would be dusk soon, too dark to see anything. The sun was just setting, and the long rays of light were stretching across the top surface of the grass.

I was crying so hard by this time that I could hardly see anything through my tears. But suddenly I noticed a little glint of light, walked over, and picked up my ring! I could hardly believe it. Mary came over and put her arms around me, and we both stood there in the parking lot, laughing and crying and hugging each other, amazed at the wonder of this little miracle.

I guess I was supposed to have that ring. It's more than just a beautiful piece of jewelry, of course. It's a symbol of love from a mother to a daughter. Someday I'll hand it down to my daughter. Hopefully she will realize how important it is, this symbol of love being passed down through the generations.

After all these years, I still wear my topaz ring every day. And I've learned my lesson! No more taking off rings away from home. When someone notices and compliments me on my ring, which happens often, I say, "Thanks, I think it's beautiful too. My Mama gave it to me."

GOT CHAINS?

We almost didn't get to the hospital.

I called the paramedics to our house in the middle of a very cold winter night and, after checking Mama out, they decided that she needed additional tests. So we called the local ambulance service and waited for them to show up. And waited. And waited. Finally, after what I considered an unreasonable amount of time, they pulled into our driveway. I'm just worried, I told myself. They're probably not so late after all and everything's going to be fine.

They strapped Mama onto the gurney, carried her out into the cold night air, and loaded her into the ambulance. As they started down the road and I followed in my Jeep, I noticed they were slipping and sliding on the ice and snow on almost every turn, and on our winding mountain road, there are a lot of turns. Then I saw that the ambulance didn't have chains! I could hardly believe it. I found out later that the reason they were late was because they had stopped en route to put on chains, only to find out that the chains they had did not fit the vehicle they were driving. So instead of going back to get a vehicle with chains (oh no, that would have been too sensible), they just showed up at our house without them.

My Jeep is fine on these slippery roads. I not only have four-wheel drive but also studded tires that track especially well on ice. I couldn't say as much for the ambulance. When we got to the "S curves" as we locally call them, and started up hill, it was a disaster waiting to happen. The ambulance slithered over to the opposite side of the road with the driver's fender scraping along the guard rail. Thank God there was a guard rail. They would have been over the side of the mountain without it! Then they came to a complete stop. On the wrong side of the road! On a blind curve!

I got out of my Jeep and marched over to the driver's window. "What in the hell is going on?" I demanded, to which the driver haughtily replied, "Step away from the vehicle! You are creating a hazard!"

Then the assistant tried to radio the fire department, but there was no reception at that point on the mountainside, so he had to get out and walk up the road to a better vantage point. I had thought it was a long time for the ambulance to get to our house. It seemed twice as long before the fire department came to our rescue. All I could think about was the fact that my helpless little Mama was trapped in that ambulance stalled on the wrong side of the road. I prayed all the time we were waiting that an out-of-control car wouldn't come sliding around our blind curve and run into us, but fortunately that didn't happen. Not too many drivers out in the wee hours of an icy, snowy night.

When the firemen did arrive, I could tell by the looks on their faces that they were incredulous at the whole situation. I heard one of them say, "What, you don't have chains?"

The only good thing about that whole insane night was that when we got to the hospital, it turned out that Mama's condition wasn't serious and we were able to come back home that same night.

In our safe four-wheel-drive studded-tires Jeep.

SAVING IT FOR GOOD

Children of the Great Depression often have a "Saving it for good" mentality. They and their families survived many long, hard years, barely managing to provide the bare necessities. As did most people in those difficult years, they made it through and lived to see better times. But when you only have one "good" dress to wear to church or for family holidays, you "save it for good." When you can rarely afford to buy a chicken or a nice piece of beef, you only serve them for a special occasion. You don't use the "good dishes" because they might get chipped. And then, years down the road when things are more plentiful, the fear still remains, the fear of doing without, of being hungry, of losing your home or not being able to afford a doctor. Those Children of the Depression carry that fear with them until the end of their days.

My own Mama had some of that same thinking. When my parents finally were able to buy their own home, every dollar had to go for necessary repairs. There was no money left over to buy new furniture. So my Mama saved dimes (dimes!) to buy a maple table and four maple chairs. She only used them a few times because she was so worried that something hot or wet would ruin the finish on the tabletop. But now with the table in place, there was no room for the folding card table where we used to eat, so we ate in the tiny kitchen. I sat at the pull-out breadboard; my brother was in his high chair; my father hunched over a tiny counter in the corner, and my Mama ate standing at the kitchen sink!

The same thinking applied to meals. Every morning it was cooked oatmeal, and on Sunday we added raisins to it. Brown-bag lunches always had peanut butter and jelly sandwiches on white bread. And every Friday night we ate creamed tuna on toast for dinner. Sunday was the special day for a roasted chicken or a beef pot roast. No one thought it was strange. It was just the way we did things.

Mama would tell us stories of how in the Depression my Grampa, her father, grew corn in his garden, dried it, packaged it in little brown bags and sold it door to door to his neighbors for popcorn. She would say if she ever had to eat cornmeal mush again she would rather starve.

In Mama's later years, after Daddy died and before she came to live with me, she became a recluse, never leaving her home. I used to drive "over the hill" to the city to visit her when I could, stopping on the way to buy her dinner at her favorite restaurant. Instead of eating out of Styrofoam boxes with plastic forks, I would take out two plates, two glasses and two silver forks from her china cabinet, over her very loud protests, and serve our food on her "good dishes." Then when we were eating on little trays in the front room, she would say, "Oh, these dishes are really pretty, aren't they?" as if she hadn't seen them before! I always washed, dried and put away every plate and fork so she wouldn't go in the kitchen and be upset all over again about two plates being in the dishwasher.

When I brought Mama up to my mountain cabin to be with me, I brought along several of her favorite pieces of furniture, as well as her "good dishes." I still use them often, as well as my own, to celebrate my gratitude for my many blessings. It gives me great pleasure to drink water from a "cranberry glass" that belonged to my Grama, to wear Mama's pearl earrings while I wash the dishes, and to sip tea from Mama's white china cup with the gold roses trim. Best of all, I like to dress up in my "good clothes" and share a meal served on the "good dishes" with my loved ones. We're not saving our special things "for good." We're enjoying them now, because the "good times" are right now.

UNINTENTIONAL MALPRACTICE

"I understand your mother is here visiting from Ohio," said the emergency-room doctor, nodding to me distractedly as if he were in a hurry to leave.

"Well, I wouldn't call it a visit; she's lived here for over 50 years," I answered, trying not to show my frustration about being required to stay in the waiting room for over two hours instead of being with Mama. "Haven't you seen her medical information chart? It was pinned to her nightgown."

I had printed out a chart showing Mama's personal information, medical history, prescriptions and current medical condition. In a large font in red ink across the top of the chart was written:

MEDICAL INFORMATION CHART
Ann LaForge
*"Patient is mentally diminished and
cannot give accurate information."*

I had shown it to the paramedics as they took Mama to the ambulance, asking that they call it to the attention of the ER staff in case I would not be allowed to go into the emergency room with her.

Mama had been admitted to the hospital in the middle of the night, gasping for air and having trouble breathing. Although she required 24-hour round-the-clock oxygen, she had been in the ER hospital bed for at least two hours without it.

I started looking for the missing chart. It was not on her bed, not on the nightstand. Finally, I spotted it lying on the ER counter – torn where it had been ripped off her clothing and crumpled like a used tissue. Why hadn't anyone read it? When

I showed it to the doctor, he said in a very irritated voice, "Well, I asked her how she was feeling and she said she was just fine." Then he turned on his heel and walked out of the room!

While waiting for the nurse to bring Mama's oxygen, and hopefully for another doctor to give her a proper examination, we could hear the sound of a young child behind the curtain in the next bed softly crying. I asked Mama if she knew what was wrong. She said she didn't know but when she had heard the little girl calling for her mother, one of the nurses went to the child's bed and told her to be quiet and stop disturbing the other patients.

Then Mama reached out, took my hand and told me quietly, "You know honey, some of these people think that just because they're on their feet and we're not, that they're better than we are." These amazing words of wisdom came from a little lady who didn't know where she lived, didn't understand her own medical condition, and sometimes didn't even recognize me, her only daughter. But she recognized Truth in a way that some intelligent, educated and respected people do not. She knew that the foundation for caring for each other is Love.

GO COMB YOUR HAIR!

LIVING WITH MAMA

"Why don't you comb your hair?" Mama said this to me in an exasperated voice, like a mother who has to tell her child over and over to do the same thing. Well, she did tell me that over and over, and was telling me again that morning. The day started out much earlier than I wanted it to, with Mama's wet bed, sponge bath, clean nightie and robe, and bed linens in the washer.

Then we were sitting in the den. Mama was wrapped in her afghan, with her oxygen and her can of Ensure. I was still in my long flannel nightgown, sipping hot tea and reading that day's inspiring message in my day book. I was trying to think about love and serenity instead of wet beds.

"Didn't you hear me? Get up and go comb your hair!" Mama said, more impatiently than ever. I wasn't playing the game right, not answering her right away, and not jumping up to do what she wanted. Usually, Mama was so sweet to me, saying "please" and "thank you" and telling me how much she appreciated me. And Mama told me all the time how pretty I was, repeatedly, day after day.

But she had a thing about my hair. I think it was because when she was young and beautiful, she wore her lovely red hair in a short, sophisticated hairstyle. Now when she was old and beautiful, she probably didn't think anyone my age should be wearing her hair with a curly, shoulder-length, comb-it-with-your-fingers kind of look. Whatever the reason, she nagged me about my hair all the time. Combing it didn't satisfy her, and neither did any explanation. But I tried again anyway. "Mama, I'm going upstairs to take a shower and shampoo my hair in a few minutes, after I finish my tea."

She kept on and on about my hair, and finally I decided not to answer her. I tried to just focus on my book and block out the sound of her grumbling. She mumbled something under her breath and then muttered, "...big, fat dummy!"

I looked up with a start! "What did you just say?"

"Nothing!"

"Did you just call me a big, fat dummy?"

"Well, so what if I did?"

I couldn't help it. I burst out laughing. "Well, that's not very nice! How come you called me a big, fat dummy?"

Mama gave her head a defiant little toss. She still had the personality to go with her red hair. With a twinkle in her eye, she said, "Well, it got your attention, didn't it? Now, are you going to go comb your hair?"

THREE HEART ATTACKS IN ONE DAY

It started in the middle of the night. Mama had a terrible pain in her chest and woke Daddy. Fortunately, he called for medical help right away. When the paramedics got to their home, Mama had another attack. She was treated and taken immediately by ambulance to the nearest local hospital. While she was being examined by the doctor, she had a third attack which stopped her heart. Mama told me later that she actually remembered being revived by "those paddles." She said it was like being hit in the chest by a truck. A big truck.

The decision was quickly made to transfer Mama to Queen of Angels Hospital which had a world-class cardiac unit. The smaller hospital was not equipped to handle a case as critical as Mama's condition.

By this time, Daddy had phoned me, and I was able to get to the hospital quickly, just as they were wheeling out the gurney to transport Mama by ambulance. When I identified myself to the attendant, he told me they didn't know if Mama would even survive the short drive to Queen of Angels. I hurried over to Mama and took her hand, trying to hold back my tears. She seemed quite alert, smiled a little and squeezed my hand. She murmured, "Don't worry, honey. I'll be just fine." Isn't it amazing that people say "Don't worry" in the most worrisome situations?

As I watched the ambulance drive off, I knew it was likely I wouldn't see Mama alive again. Daddy and I drove together to Queen of Angels. Daddy was holding up pretty well, considering what he had been through that morning. When we got to the hospital, it took forever for us to find out anything about Mama's condition and prognosis. It was agonizing not knowing if she was going to live or die. Daddy told me quietly, "I don't know what I'll do if I lose her."

I couldn't think of anything to say to console him; I was so frightened too. So, I just reminded him, "Mama's in the best hands here, Daddy, the best in the country. We just have to trust that they know what to do to help her."

During Mama's hospitalization, the Swan-Ganz procedure, a new treatment at that time, was performed by Dr. Ganz himself. Although Mama later credited Dr. Ganz with "saving her life," that may not have been completely accurate. It was the combination of the results from that procedure, the diagnosis of her condition, appropriate treatment, and medication that was responsible for enabling her to return to health.

After she was moved out of the ICU and into a private room, Mama asked Daddy to bring her the makeup bag from her purse. We knew she was getting better when she started to think about how she looked. I had gone over to be with Daddy and drive him to the hospital when he got Mama's purse from their bedroom and opened it. There, in addition to the makeup case and her keys, was a package of cigarettes! We both just stared at it, dumbfounded.

The doctor had been telling Mama for several years that her smoking was damaging her heart. Although she was only in her mid-fifties, she had all the symptoms: shortness of breath, heart palpitations, weakness, occasional dizziness. We were worried about her and begged her to stop smoking, and she told us she had. She even told her doctor she had quit, but right before our eyes was the proof that she had not quit, and worse yet, she had lied about it.

It was the only time in my life that I ever saw Daddy really angry at Mama; I mean really mad. He adored my mother, would do anything for her to make her happy, worshiped the ground she walked on, as they used to say in those days.

Daddy just stood there for several seconds, staring at those cigarettes. Then he yanked the package out of her purse and started pulling the cigarettes out of the wrapper and tearing them into little pieces. All the time he was muttering, incoherently, about how she had promised him, and how she had lied to him, and how she had almost killed herself, and all because of these damned cigarettes!

When he finished ripping up all the cigarettes, he grabbed his jacket and, forgetting about the makeup case, started for the front door, saying, "Come on, Lynney, we're going to the damn hospital!" And I thought to myself, it's a good thing I'm the one who's driving. He wouldn't be safe behind the wheel!

When we got to the hospital, Daddy marched into Mama's room and, without so much as a "Hello," started in on her: how dare she lie to him, and how dare she lie to her own doctor, for God's sake, and were her damn cigarettes more important to her than everyone who loved her, more important than he was, her own husband? He was so riled up and was talking so loudly that the nurse came in and reminded him that Mama was in a fragile condition and he would either have to calm down or leave.

Mama was crying by this time, not even saying anything, just crying. I left the room and let them talk together in private. I guess they reached some sort of agreement because Daddy came out of her room a short time later, looking tired and old, and said, "Let's go home, Lynney." I hurried in to Mama, hugged and kissed her and told her I loved her. She was still crying, but quietly, and managed to say she loved me too.

I don't know if it was because of Daddy or because she almost died, really almost died, but she never smoked a single cigarette after that. Not one.

But she was still her feisty self, even after her ordeal. The doctor told her she had to change her diet and start exercising regularly, every day. He told her to start by walking around the block and work up to walking a mile a day. She told her doctor, and us, that she had never voluntarily walked a mile in her life and she wasn't about to start now. And as for her diet, anyone could see by her trim figure that her "diet" was working just fine.

And she lived to the ripe old age of 87. Go figure!

THE QUEEN ON HER THRONE

LIVING WITH MAMA

I was in the shower, enjoying my few minutes of privacy, when I heard Mama downstairs, calling me; "Lynne, Lynne!" It was like having a newborn baby in the house; there was no such thing as an uninterrupted shower, or an uninterrupted night's sleep, for that matter.

"Lynne!" Louder now, more insistent.

Oh, I don't want to get out of this shower yet. The hot water feels so good...

"LYNNE!" She was screaming then.

What in the world is going on down there? Has she hurt herself? Has she fallen? I rinsed off as fast as I could, wrapped myself in a towel, and rushed downstairs. I found Mama in the downstairs bathroom, sitting on the toilet, perfectly fine, except that she was furious.

She had completely forgotten the original reason she wanted me, but as soon as she saw me, she screamed at me at the top of her voice, "Where have you been?!" Didn't you hear me calling you?!"

I said, "Mama, I was in the shower." Then she was really exasperated with me. "And how was I supposed to know that?"

"Well, you can hear the water running." But even as I said those words, I knew Mama was past the point where she could understand the connection between the sound of the running water and my being in the shower. "Mama, what do you want? I'm dripping all over the floor."

She straightened herself up in her most regal manner. Now, it's hard to look regal when you're 86 years old, 95 pounds, sitting on the toilet in your nightgown, with your incontinence pad down around your ankles. But she pulled it off pretty well; she gave me, the impudent peasant, her most disparaging look, and in her best "let them eat cake" voice, said to me, **"WELL, JUST DRIP!"**

AGAIN

"We were hit." Those are the words Mama had written in her journal, followed by a brief description of how they were robbed. The words seem so calm and ordinary, written on a page or seen in print, but they're anything but calm. They're terrifying and frustrating and life-changing.

It was early on a Saturday evening and Mama and Daddy were coming home from church. It was easier for them to go out in the afternoon than it was to get up and get going on a Sunday morning. As Daddy parked the car in front of their house, another car pulled in behind them. Daddy had the first stages of dementia then and although he could still drive, he was, as he said, "movin' kinda slow." Mama got out of the car ahead of him and started to walk up the sidewalk.

A young man got out of the car behind, called to my Mama and started asking her for directions to a nearby location. When she stopped to help him, he walked up to her, pulled a knife, pointed it at her, and demanded her purse. When she handed it to him, he looked at her hands and said, "And your jewelry too." Mama gave him her wristwatch and then she started to cry. With tears running down her face, she begged him, "Please, please let me keep my wedding ring." It was a modest gold band with tiny diamond chips across the top, purchased decades ago in post-depression years with a few hard-earned dollars. Mama had never had it off her hand. That man put the point of his knife to my Mama's neck, pressed hard enough to make a trickle of blood start dripping down, and said, "Ya wanna die, lady? Ya wanna die?" She gave him the ring.

Meanwhile Daddy was still sitting in the car, oblivious to what was happening. Another man walked over to him, yanked open the car door and demanded his wallet and wedding ring.

Daddy gave him his wallet, which had quite a bit of cash in it. But he couldn't give them his ring because he had arthritis in his hands and his knuckles were swollen. It was only later we realized that Daddy was fortunate they didn't cut his finger off.

What can you do when something like that happens to someone you love? Well, there's not much. Call them on the phone. Try to console them. Tell them how much you care. Tell your friends how angry and helpless you feel. Not much.

I remember a conversation I had with Daddy some months after the robbery. We were sitting in their front room and it was a warm day. As I got up to open the door to let in some fresh air, Daddy said quickly, "Lynney, don't! Don't open the door." He went on to explain that they had thought they lived in a safe, quiet neighborhood, but now he and Mama were afraid to leave the door open with just the security screen, even in broad daylight. "You know," he said, "you read about this kind of thing in the newspaper happening all the time, and hear about it on television. But it's never real until it happens to you. I feel so angry at myself that I couldn't protect your mother, but I don't know what I could have done. And we know they're still out there."

They did indeed know. Shortly after the robbery, Daddy was in the alley behind their house, bringing the trash cans out of the garage for the next day pick-up, when a car came speeding down the alley. It was the robbers! One of the men leaned out the window and hollered at my Daddy, "Hey Pops, how ya doin'?" Whether he was just taunting Daddy or whether he didn't recognize him, we don't know. But it kept the fear alive.

• • • • •

Time had passed and the memory of the robbery had faded somewhat. It was late afternoon and Mama returned home from grocery shopping. Daddy wasn't home that day and the house was empty. Mama parked the car, got out, picked up some packages, and walked up to the front door. She put her key into the doorknob and opened the door part-way. Then she thought, *if I leave the car in the street out front, I'll just have to come back later to put it in the garage.* So, she closed the door, went back, drove the car around to the alley and parked it in the garage. As she was closing the garage door, she noticed that the back gate was ajar. *That's funny,* she thought, *we always keep that gate bolted.* She walked over to close the gate, looked down at the ground and there was the wastebasket from her bedroom. It was filled with silverware, jewelry and other small valuables! She had interrupted a robbery! A robbery!

Again!

A later inventory of the house revealed a stolen television and microwave and several other unimportant and replaceable things. But the saddest thing to lose was Daddy's collection of custom-made rifles. Every gun was a work of art, taking years of work and Daddy's remarkable artistic talent to create. Now they were in the hands of criminals.

The greatest blessing, however, was the fact that Mama had not walked in on the robbers. If she had, there is no telling what could have happened. Fortunately, she was safe.

This time.

• • • • •

Daddy's dementia continued to advance on its inexorable path. He became more unstable, weaker and often confused. It became more and more difficult for him to get up from his chair. If Mama went out for a quick trip to the grocery store and I happened to call while she was gone, it took Daddy a long time to get up to answer the phone.

So, for Father's Day I bought Daddy a cordless phone. It was a very simple device, a green "on" button and a red "off" button and big numbers. But no matter how I explained it, he wasn't able to use the phone. Finally, he said, "You have to understand, Lynney. I've got too much stuff in my head and it's all mixed up in there. When I was young, we had horse-drawn buggies instead of cars and outhouses instead of indoor plumbing. We grew our own food and made our own clothes and wrote letters because we didn't have a phone. I've seen so much change that I don't have any room in my head for more." So, I told him, "I do understand, Daddy," and I hugged and kissed him. After returning home, I took the phone back to the store.

And then one night Daddy went to bed, slowly, but still walking and talking, and when he woke up the next morning he could do neither. A horrendous day followed of ambulances, hospitals, and doctors. They decided to keep Daddy at the hospital for observation and then make arrangements to move him to a nursing home.

My Mama was a strong, resilient woman. She handled the crisis well, making what decisions were necessary for Daddy's care. But at the end of the day, she was alone... in that empty house. It was probably one of the few times she and Daddy had been apart in all the decades they were married. As she lay in her bed that night, she kept saying to herself, "I'm going to be fine. I'm going to be okay."

That's when she heard the breaking glass. Someone was breaking into the house! She realized with dismay that with the confusion of the day she had forgotten to set the house alarm. She listened to more smashing and then men's voices. Then, even more frightening, footsteps coming down the hall. It was her nightmare all over again: two men, coming through the doorway, holding knives.

They grabbed hold of her, yanked her out of bed, and demanded that she show them where her jewelry was. Even in such terrifying circumstances she managed to keep her wits. Knowing that her good jewelry was now put away in a place where they weren't likely to find it, she gave them her cheap costume jewelry and some of Daddy's less-valuable things. And off they went, carrying the microwave and the television.

Again.

Mama called me the next morning and calmly told me she had been robbed, and asked me if I could take her shopping for a microwave. She told me she used to think she didn't want a microwave, but now she used it to reheat her coffee. When I went to pick her up, I was incredulous at how she seemed to be taking all of this in stride. I told her so, but she said everything would work out fine. My brother Jim was moving back in again. She was getting another microwave, another television, and she didn't care about that costume jewelry anyway.

"The most important thing," she started to say, and then her calm façade evaporated in a flood of tears. "The most important thing," she struggled on, "is that they didn't rape me."

I held her and patted her and tried to calm her, saying quietly, "Well Mama, a lady your age...

The fierce look on her face stopped me mid-sentence. "Lynne, you should know that men like that, who don't even deserve to be called men, monsters like that have no respect for women, or for age, or for human life. They respect nothing and there is nothing they wouldn't do. Nothing."

RULES

"Ohhhh!" I groaned, as I dragged myself up from the depths of sleep, rolled over, still tucked underneath my warm down comforter, and tried to focus one eye on my bedside clock. It read 4:20 a.m. "Oh no!" I dropped my head back down onto my pillow. Immediately I felt the delicious and enticing mist of slumber start floating around me.

But only for a second or two. Then I heard again the sound that woke me in the first place: Mama's voice, calling loudly and insistently from somewhere downstairs, "Lynne. Lynne!"

I opened my eyes again. It seemed to take even more effort to get myself to some level of consciousness.

But my little dog Annie had already abandoned her post as official foot warmer, jumped from the end of my bed, and was racing back and forth from the top of the stairs to my bedside, as if to say, "Come on, Mom! Grama's calling us!"

And indeed, she was, even louder... or maybe I could just hear her better when I was finally awake. Her voice floated up the stairwell, insistent, exasperated, like a boss complaining to a worker about poor service. "Ly-ynne!"

I sat up, pulled on my fleece-lined slippers and slipped into my robe. Downstairs I found Mama, not in her bed, or in the bathroom, but sitting in her chair in the den, in the dark. As I turned on a lamp, I saw her in her flannel nightgown and slippers, wrapped and covered with an assortment of afghans and chair covers, trying to keep warm in the cool night air.

In my sleep-walking state I blurted out, "Mama, what are you doing up?"

She gave me an indignant look. "What do you mean, 'What am I doing?' I'm waiting for you!"

I realized that Mama didn't have any conception of time; literally couldn't tell night from day. So, I patted her on the arm, gave her my best attempt at a smile and told her, "I know, Mama. I know." As I unwrapped all the layers, helped her to her feet and started walking her back to her bed, I decided to try logic. "Mama, look out the window. It's pitch black out. It's nighttime. The house is cold. There aren't any lights on. I was in bed and you need to be in bed too. You need to stay tucked in here in your nice warm bed until you can look out the window and see that it's daylight."

By then she was sitting on the edge of her bed. She gave me one more "look" to show me how displeased she was with me, yanked off her slippers, and as I was tucking her into bed, she complained loudly, "I don't know how you expect me to live with all your complicated rules!"

I LOVE YOU, DADDY

"Why are my father's arms tied down?" my brother, Jim, demanded, as we walked into Daddy's room at the convalescent hospital.

The plump, middle-aged nurse standing near the bed glanced over at us and explained, "Well, ya see, that's to stop him from pullin' out this here feedin' tube."

"But we didn't order a feeding tube! We don't want him on a feeding tube!" I looked to Mama for agreement and she nodded her head as she stared at Daddy, a troubled look on her face.

Daddy was lying in the hospital bed, his head and shoulders elevated, eyes closed, moving about restlessly. He didn't seem to be awake but he was moaning softly and pulling helplessly at his wrist restraints. He had a horrible-looking black plastic tube sticking out of his mouth. As I imagined a tube like that, running down my throat, I felt like choking.

"Well, ya see," the nurse went on, "he needs to have this here feedin' tube because it takes just way too long to spoon feed him now. It takes like a half hour just to get a bowl of soup..."

"I don't care how long it takes to feed him. I want that tube out, now!" Jim's voice was getting louder as he was getting more upset.

Before the nurse could reply, I put a restraining hand on Jim's arm and said, "Come on, Jim, let's go back to the front desk and talk to someone in charge."

Jim gave the nurse an angry look, as if this were all her fault, turned on his heel, and marched out of the room, followed by me and Mama.

It took a very long time, talking to this, that, and the next person in charge. We banged at the gates of "hospital procedure" for quite a while. Jim and I were getting nowhere when Mama finally spoke up.

She stood up from her chair, all 5 feet, 95 pounds of her and, quivering slightly with her old age tremor, she looked calmly at Head Guy, sitting behind his expensive desk in his fancy office, wearing his custom-tailored three-piece suit. She said quietly but clearly, "Sir, I realize that you have many responsibilities here in this hospital, but I have only one responsibility. That is to my husband of fifty years. We are coming to the end of our days now. He is coming to the end of his life. It is not our wish to prolong his life" (she glanced at me and Jim to include us) "and we don't hold you responsible for doing so. What we do want is for his last days to be as comfortable as possible and this is what we, his family, do hold you and your staff responsible for. I am asking you, sir, to please allow my husband to die comfortably and peacefully."

That gentleman sat behind his desk for several seconds, apparently stunned. Then he spoke gently and respectfully: "Of course, Mrs., uh (he looked down at our paperwork,) Mrs. LaForge. I'll take care of it."

And he did.

The next time that Mama and I went to visit Daddy, he was sleeping peacefully, no wrist restraints, no horrible feeding tube. We talked to him quietly, held his hand, and smoothed his hair back from his brow. He hadn't been fully awake or able to recognize us for weeks. He murmured quietly but didn't seem to know we were there, so after a short visit we decided to leave.

I leaned over him and kissed him on the forehead and said, "Good-bye, Daddy. I love you." And then Mama kissed him and told him she loved him too.

We walked to the door of the room, and just as I started to pull the door open, we heard a voice behind us. We both turned around and to our amazement, Daddy was partly sitting up in bed, propped up on one elbow. He raised his other arm up in the air over his head, waved his hand and said clearly, "I love you."

Mama rushed back over to him, put her arms around him, kissed him, and said, "I love you too, Stephen."

I stood there at the door, watching the two of them, almost feeling like an intruder. So I stayed there, my hand on the door handle, and called over, "I love you, Daddy." And he looked at me, smiled a little and said, "I love you too, Lynney."

Those were his last words. He slipped away that night, comfortably and peacefully, just as we had hoped.

MY LOVELY PRISON

LIVING WITH MAMA

I read that expression, a "lovely prison," in my Family Chronicle, written by my great-aunt Effie. My great-grandmother said it about living on the family farm, far away from town, isolated from her friends, community, and activities. Now, down through all these generations, I know how she felt, even though I never knew her, except for some old black and white photographs and a few words written on paper, now yellowed with age.

I'm sure she loved her home. The pictures of the farm look exactly like our idea of "life in the good old days." It was a large, charming farmhouse with big porches, the place for family gatherings of dignified-looking men with their neatly trimmed beards, dressed up in their best suits. There were pretty women in long white summer dresses, holding darling babies on their laps, and boys in old-fashioned knickers, romping on the lawn under the big trees. A wonderful life, happy and serene... and I'm sure it was, in some ways. But the days that stretched out between those family get-togethers must have been long and lonely for my great-grandmother.

I feel that same sense of imprisonment in the midst of beauty as I sit here tonight, writing these words in my journal. I can hardly see the paper for blinking back tears, trying to understand my feelings of sadness at the end of what has been a very lovely day.

I don't live on a country farm, but my log cabin home in the mountains is just as wonderful to me. I love the view out my windows of my rose garden, the sweet aroma of pine forests and the snow-capped peaks. Indoors, I'm surrounded by lace curtains and family pictures, pretty and comfortable furniture that I've collected over a lifetime. Tonight, I ate my homemade potato soup from a lovely blue and white china bowl, and poured my tea from a darling little silver teapot that belonged to my grandmother.

I live in the midst of beauty, but I'm trapped here. Or at least I have the feeling of being trapped, imprisoned by responsibility, by obligation, and by love.

Yes, by love. My invalid mother sits here in the room with me, with her sweet smiling face, wearing her pretty blue robe, warmly wrapped up against the chill of the evening. But this isn't really my mother. My real mother slipped away from me long ago, bit by bit, leaving in her place this dependent little child. And like a little child, she is constantly demanding my time and attention. She needs more orange juice, she wants cookies, will I bring her a Kleenex, her afghan needs to be straightened, her robe isn't right, her fingers are sticky, she needs a washcloth, where is the bathroom, help her up from her chair, hold her arm, she doesn't know where the bathroom is. She is clutching at my sleeve, whimpering, pleading with me because she doesn't know which way to walk to find the bathroom.

It exhausts me to write these words; it exhausts me to live like this. I feel like I'm drowning, buffeted this way and that by the storm of my own emotions: sadness, sympathy, frustration, guilt, love.

I love my Mama dearly. I hate the fact that I sometimes feel impatient with her. She is so sweet, always complimenting me, always thanking me for every little thing.

As I pour out my feelings on paper, I can feel peace start to settle down around me. And the life lesson in all this starts to become clear, as if appearing through a fog. A grateful heart.

Be grateful for my Mama, for her giving me my very life, for caring for me all those years, for showing me her example of giving thanks, despite her infirmity and failing health, for every favor and every blessing.

My Family Chronicle goes on to say that my great-grandmother learned to love the farm despite her loneliness. Because of her great love and interest in everything, her children, her books, her flowers, she could not stay unhappy, but could only live in Gratitude.

[My "Lovely" Log Cabin Home]

THE OTHER LADY

I yelled at Mama, really yelled at her.

I was out in the yard, watering the rosebushes, enjoying the beautiful autumn weather, when I heard her calling me with that insistent, worried tone in her voice, like a little kid who wakes up and doesn't know where her mother is. I knew she had wakened from her nap and was out on the porch, even before I walked around the corner of the house and saw her standing there in her nightgown and slippers, shaking with that old age tremor, holding onto the banister at the top of the stairs for support. As soon as she saw me, Mama tried to take a step down, lost her balance, and would have fallen down the entire flight of stairs if I hadn't been there to catch her.

I managed to get us turned around and back up to the porch, then into the house. Relief and exhaustion swept over me. I had been awake since four o'clock that morning, with Mama calling and calling up to my bedroom for me to come down and keep her company since she was "all alone down here."

Fear and frustration welled up inside me and exploded in a torrent of words: "How many times have I told you not to open this front door? A hundred times! You must not open this front door!"

Mama looked up at me with a bewildered expression and said, "But why, honey?"

Honey, she's calling me honey after I just yelled at her. I started to feel ashamed of myself and tried to backtrack, explaining that our little dog, Annie, would get out, and wouldn't we feel terrible if something happened to Annie? I certainly couldn't tell Mama that I thought I didn't even trust her out on the front porch.

Later that evening, Mama told me she didn't know what she was doing wrong, but she just couldn't seem to "get along with the people around here." Knowing full well that I was "the people around here," I felt even more guilty.

When I tucked her into bed that night, she grabbed my hand, gave me a timid little smile, and said, "You're not mad at me, are you?"

I patted her hand and said softly, "No, Mama, I'm not mad at you. I love you." But in my heart I said, "Dear God, I'm so sorry. Please forgive me!"

The next morning when she woke up, I went into her room and said, "Hi, Mama, how are you doing?"

And she looked at me without a glimmer of recognition of who I was and asked: "Are you the nice lady?"

Oh, she still remembers me yelling at her. It made my heart ache, but I smiled, and lied to her and said, "Yes, Mama, I'm the nice lady."

Looking relieved, she said, "Well, I hope that other lady doesn't come back anymore. She says mean things to me!"

Feeling like a hypocrite, I asked her, "What does the mean lady say to you?"

And Mama answered, "Well, she told me I was a stupid little worm!"

A stupid little worm! Dear God! What could one say to another human being that would be more dehumanizing than to call them a stupid – little – worm!

Although Mama didn't have the words to tell me, she saw through my excuse about not letting the dog out. On some level, she understood that I did consider her incompetent, and although I never actually called her a stupid little worm, I was treating her with disrespect.

Somewhere beyond her inability to tell night from day, to walk down stairs safely, or even to recognize her own daughter, some place past that barrier is the mother that I know and respect and love with all my heart.

I put my arms around her, gave her a long hug, and told her, "Don't worry, Mama, that other lady isn't coming back."

DEAR GOD,
PLEASE GIVE ME PATIENCE

When Mama wakes me up
for the fifth time tonight,
Dear God
Please give me Patience.

When I ask her why she called me
And she says, "I just wanted to see you, honey."
Dear God
Please let me hear her with Patience.

When I tell her,
"Mama, you have to quit waking me up.
I'm tired and I have to get some sleep."
Dear God
Please help me speak
with love and Patience.

When she says, "Oh, honey, I'm so sorry.
I promise not to wake you up again."
And I know she won't remember
And will probably call me again
As soon as I get back in my bed.

·

·

·

Dear God
Please, please
give me Patience.

(I wrote this prayer sometime in the middle of the night,
in a notebook I kept beside my bed.)

YOU'RE NUTS!

During the years of caring for Mama, I realized I was very fortunate. The mood swings and erratic behavior that often accompany dementia were few and far between. But as time went by, her ability to make sense of her surroundings was diminished and her mood swings occurred more often.

One evening at bedtime, I went over to Mama's chair where she was sitting watching television and said, "Time for bed, Mama." I took off her oxygen, and tried to help her stand up.

She yanked her arm away from me and said, "What are you doing?" I told her I was just helping her up, and then she said suspiciously, "Where are you taking me?" I told her we're going to the bathroom, and she insisted she didn't have to go. After much coaxing, I finally got her to the bathroom, and started to untie her robe. "No, no, I don't want to take off my robe!" she said as she clutched it frantically.

"It's such a pretty robe, Mama, and I know how much you like it. We're just going to hang it up carefully so it won't get wrinkled and will be waiting for you in the morning." She finally, reluctantly, allowed me to take it off of her.

Every little step was met with resistance and anxiety: no, she doesn't want to get into bed; no, don't take off her slippers; where are you putting her slippers, how will she find them when she gets up; her nightgown is rumpled; her pillow is too low; she needs a Kleenex; she needs a drink; she wants a cookie; where am I going, don't leave.

But then she gave me her sweet smile, told me I'm so pretty, thanked me for everything I did for her, and told me she loved me.

I felt like I'd gone back decades in time, trying to get my own little children tucked into bed. It was always one more drink or one more bedtime story. But back then it was just the cute, normal procrastination of kids so full of life and energy that they didn't want to give up at the end of the day. With Mama, she was like a little child too, sometimes happy, but sometimes confused and worried about what was going to happen next.

Usually, I tried to keep her to a familiar routine so she didn't get too confused or upset, and things went along smoothly.

But sometimes I was too tired to even keep track of time. One night I awoke about 1:00 a.m., finding myself still in the den, crunched up in my chair, television blaring. I had fallen asleep there, exhausted, because Mama had wakened me several times the night before. Sleep deprivation is an insidious thing, robbing you of energy and mental alertness.

I got up, muscles cramped and aching, dragged myself over to Mama's chair and said, "Come on, Mama, let's go to bed." Over her loud protestations, I gently lifted her up and slowly steered her toward the bathroom. My usual cajoling had no effect as I tried to take off her robe. She started yelling, and then screaming, louder and louder, "No, no, I'm not taking off my robe! Let me go sit down! I'm not going to bed! Let me out of here! Leave me alone!"

By this time I was thinking, I'm so glad I don't have neighbors close by. They would have called the authorities for suspected elder abuse!

"Mama," I said quietly, "calm down. We just need to go to bed."

"I'm not going to bed! Let me out of here! Leave me alone!" Mama struggled to get past me and through the bathroom doorway.

"I'm not going to leave you alone. We're getting ready for bed," I said as patiently and gently as possible.

As I tried again to take off her robe, she started swinging at me, flailing her thin little arms, and shrieking, "**HELP, HELP!**"

Help? Who does she think could help her?

"Mama, please quiet down! There's nobody here but you and me, and I'm trying to help you."

"**HELP! HELP ME! HELP!**" She whirled around and glared up at me. I'm only two inches taller than she is, but I suddenly felt like a huge predator, facing my cornered but ferocious little prey. She jutted out her chin, squinted her eyes and said in her most scathing tone, "You know what's the matter with you? **YOU'RE NUTS!**"

"Mama, please!"

"You're **NUTS! YOU'RE NUTS!**"

I don't even remember the rest of the evening. I got her to bed somehow, got myself to bed, had an unbroken night's sleep for a change, and the next day life went on as usual.

But I kept thinking of her accusation: YOU'RE NUTS! Yes, maybe I am nuts. Sometimes I feel like a virtual prisoner in my own home, caring for Mama these last several years. I've given up huge chunks of my life, my freedom, missing time with friends and with my music outings, even family gatherings, when Mama wasn't feeling well enough to go out or I couldn't get caregivers for her. And for what? For a woman that doesn't bear any resemblance to my mother, especially mentally, a woman who doesn't even know me most of the time. Why am I doing this? Why?

Well, I guess I know why. Because I love her with all my heart, and I just can't give her up, that's why. I can't give her up to strangers, no matter how professional they may be, people who wouldn't love her as I do, or care if she was confused or anxious. I just can't let her go, or at least I can't let her go until I know she'll be safe and happy, and at peace with God.

THE DEATH CARDS

I am not a superstitious person. I don't worry about black cats crossing my path, or whether it's Friday the 13th. I respect other people's beliefs in astrology and horoscopes and such things, but I don't believe in them myself. So, years ago, while at a weekend party, a woman friend of ours offered to read Tarot cards, I joined in, just for the fun of it. We sat in a circle and the reader, whose name was Barbara, offered the cards to each of us in turn. We would shuffle, draw several cards, and arrange them in a certain pattern. Then Barbara would explain what the cards meant and how they would affect us. The cards revealed an assortment of good and bad fortunes. The "good" news was received by the women in our circle with laughter and joking, and the "bad" news was met with groans and sympathy. As I looked around at my circle of friends, I found myself wondering how many of them really believed in the ability of Tarot cards to predict the future, and how many, like myself, looked at it as an amusing party game.

Then my turn came. I shuffled, drew out my cards, and laid them in front of me. Barbara gasped, staring at the cards, and several of the other ladies who were familiar with the Tarot began to whisper among themselves. All of the cards I had drawn represented change, endings, and death. Barbara told me that because my sign is Scorpio, all these events would come in threes, but she hastened to assure me that the death cards didn't necessarily mean the death of a person. They could mean, she said, the end of being in one place or a change in a relationship. She didn't sound very convincing however. I could tell she was actually worried, as were several of my other friends. Well, I thought, I know some of these ladies really believe in fortune-telling but I don't, and it's not going to worry me.

Several months later, I went on a day trip with a girlfriend to a nearby mountain community. I had dreamed of living in the mountains all of my adult life. When I saw the town and the area, I fell in love with everything, thought maybe my dream could come true, and started planning how I could arrange to move there. At one point in the transition, the old memory of those "death" cards came back to me. If I believed in those cards, which I don't, this would be the first ending: the ending of thirty-five years of being in our family home in the city. But of course, I don't believe in those cards, so forget it! Which I did.

For a while.

When I finally moved to my dream cabin in the mountains, I brought with me my dear little black dog, Annie, and my wonderful cat, Jack. Annie, of course, was the perfect dog, and Jack was the best cat I have ever had. He was a big boy, part Burmese, and so handsome with his thick shiny grey coat fluffed out around him. His amber eyes shone with love as he looked up at me, quietly waiting for a word, a pat, or maybe a treat. He was very affectionate, always wanting to be near me, following me around from room to room.

Shortly after we moved in, as I was busy getting unpacked, I noticed that Jack stopped eating, just quit completely. Then he stopped following me, too. Desperately worried about him, I took him to a nearby vet, spent hundreds upon hundreds of dollars that I couldn't afford, all for useless treatments that only prolonged the agony of his last days. It was so shocking, so sudden, and it saddened the joy of the first weeks in my new home. And then, I remembered the death cards. Is this number two? Is Jack's death number two? Will there be a number three? Lynne, I scolded myself, stop thinking like that!

Little did I know.

• • • • •

Weeks went by, a few short months. I was busy, busy and so happy, commuting to my city house to teach music and pack boxes, then driving back to my cabin to unpack and settle in.

I was in the city that day... when I got the call. I had just finished teaching a lesson and was expecting another student soon when the phone rang. It was my mother's bath nurse. She wanted to know when I was coming to see my Mama. When I said I was planning to see her the next day, she told me calmly but firmly that I really needed to come today, soon, now. I had never gotten a call from her before, had never met her in person. When I asked her if Mama was okay, she said, yes, she was fine, but there were a few things that really had to be taken care of right away. As I made the hour-long trip from my city house to Mama's home, thoughts were flying through my head. I remembered a conversation I had with Mama just that morning. When I phoned her to tell her I was coming to see her the next day, she asked me if I would bring her some orange juice. I asked her if my brother Jim, who was living with her at the time, had bought her orange juice, she said yes, he usually does, but she didn't have any. So, of course I told her I would get some. But it seemed odd.

When I arrived, the nurse met me on the front porch. We introduced ourselves politely as strangers do when they meet in person for the first time. And that was the last normal thing I did for the rest of that day, or for that week, or for a long time after that. That kind lady had the good sense to wait until I made the drive safely across town, before telling me that my brother Jim was dead... sitting on the sofa in the attached apartment in the back of my parents' home. Moreover, when she had been there the previous week to bathe Mama, the house had smelled strongly of something dead. Probably a rodent, she had thought. But there was no mistaking the smell now. It almost knocked me to my knees as she and I went back in through the front door.

Mama was sitting in the front room looking a little worried. And the thought hit me, *Oh Mama, how long have you been sitting here by yourself? How long have you been going hungry and thirsty?* I gave her a hug and a kiss and told her that everything was fine. Then, like a robot, I walked through the front room, the dining area, the kitchen, the laundry room, and through the half-open door into the back apartment.

Jim had been dead, in that room, for two weeks. Decades have passed since that afternoon, but I remember it like it was last week. I had nightmares for years, flashbacks during the days. There are no words... no words.

I was thrown into a whirlwind of shock and confusion. I remember saying to the nurse, "What should we do?" And she said calmly, "Honey, you need to call the police." Dazed, I said "Oh, yes, of course." The police came, and the coroner, and the grief counselors. I didn't know how Mama was going to take the news, but when I told her "that man" that she had seen in the back apartment was her son, Jim, and he was dead, she said in a very conversational tone of voice that she knew something must be wrong, because it wasn't like Jim not to come and see her. I thanked God for her dementia that day, because it spared her the grief of losing her only son, and the horror of his death.

There was, as the police put it, "evidence of foul play." Jim's cause of death was uncertain. The house had been unlocked for probably about two weeks. I shuddered to think of Mama living in an unlocked house in that high-risk neighborhood. Mama's Cadillac had been stolen, as well as her credit cards and checkbook. As time went by, forged checks in the amount of many thousands of dollars appeared on bank statements. Mama's credit cards had been used for extravagant spending sprees.

The police wrote their reports. The coroner took Jim's body. Sometime in the confusion, the bath nurse left. I didn't have a chance to thank that kind lady. The grief counselors, who were volunteers, wives of policemen and firemen, stayed with us, talking for quite a while, I guess until they thought I was clear-minded enough to handle things. Then they left, and Mama and I were alone.

I tried to get my wits together. First things first. The house was uninhabitable and I had to get Mama out of there, that day. Of course, she didn't want to go. At that time, she was a recluse who never left her home for any reason. I packed a few things, and we went to my city house. Then for the next few days Mama stayed with my friend Terri, while I ran around like a crazy person dealing with police, family, Jim's funeral, banks, fumigators, and locksmiths.

When Mama and I finally left town and started home to my cabin in the mountains, I had the most bizarre sense of relief, as if I had been let out of an insane asylum and was free to go. It was nighttime when we arrived, and it had snowed that day. The moonlight was glistening white everywhere, like a fairyland. It was so – very – beautiful! And I was so glad to be home that tears of gratitude ran down my face.

Mama wasn't happy being there that night, but in a day or so she forgot her old home. Imagine that! Forgetting the home you have lived in for half a century! And she forgot about Jim being dead, too. One day she told me, as if I didn't know, as if he weren't my brother, "I have a son named Jim." And suddenly I remembered the death cards. Was this number three? "Stop it, Lynne!" I told myself. But I couldn't stop it. It was in my head now. Was this number three? Was number one the end of my time living in the city? Was number two the death of my dear cat, Jack? Was number three this horrific death of my only brother, my darling Jimmy, our golden boy? Please God, let this be the end of it. And then I heard myself praying to God to end a superstition that didn't exist. But that didn't matter, and God didn't hear me anyway. That wasn't the end of it.

The worst was yet to come.

• • • • •

The next few weeks tumbled by in a series of crises, one after another. Mama was in fragile health and was in and out of hospitals. There were doctors and hospital staff and prescriptions and medical equipment. There were realtors and attorneys and impound lot owners and police officers and bank officials and credit card companies. And there was paperwork. Unending and everlasting paperwork.

Then there was Mama's house. It was filled with fifty years' worth of stuff and had to be emptied and sold. I kept some of

Mama's favorite things that were special to me, and things that Mama would recognize as familiar. My son Michael, God bless him, helped me move things, dump things, sell things.

Our family helped me hold an estate sale. That day, I was talking to Mama's next-door neighbor, and he told me a sad little story. Some weeks before, he had been out mowing his front lawn, when he saw Mama standing on her front porch with her pocketbook in her hands. She waved him over, gave him a five-dollar bill, all the money she had in her purse, and asked him if he would go to McDonalds and buy her cheese-burgers. Kind man that he was, he did just that, bringing her five cheeseburgers. How could he know she had no food in the house? In his wildest dreams he couldn't have imagined that Jimmy was dead in the backroom. He just thought she was an eccentric old lady. He told me how sorry he was, and wished he had done more.

On top of all this, I wasn't completely moved out of my city house yet. I was moving from our large home where we raised our big family to a much smaller cabin, and had many deci-sions to make about what to keep and what to sell, give away, or throw away.

Mama and I drove to the city for what I hoped was a last "moving trip." Mama stayed at Terri's house again. How could I have gotten through all this turmoil without Terri's help? My son Ken and I rented a moving van. I had been packing, moving, and unpacking for months now. Ken had been my strong right arm all the way through. He and I went to my city house and loaded up the last of the last of my stuff. Now all that remained was to make the drive back up the mountain, unload the van and return it, and I was officially "moved in." Finally.

In celebration, we ordered take-out from our favorite Mexican restaurant, and phoned Ken's 17-year-old daughter, Cheyenne, to drive over and join us. The three of us sat cross-legged on the bare wood floor, laughing and talking and enjoying our meal. When it was time for us to leave, Ken and I tried to talk Cheyenne into riding up the mountain with us. "You could sleep in the canopy bed in the guest room. You know how you love that bed," I cajoled her. But she said no, she would come up soon with Ken to visit, but that night her friends were waiting for her and she was late already. If only we could have changed her mind.

If only.

And then... the call came, the phone ringing loudly in my mountain kitchen. Ken and I had been up all night and had just finished emptying the last things out of the van. We were sitting, tired but happy, at my table, eating left-over Mexican food. I answered the phone. My daughter-in-law Robin was on the line, telling us that Cheyenne was in the hospital. She had been beaten by an ex-boyfriend, was in a coma, and was not expected to live.

Ken went flying back down the mountain, with me calling after him to be careful. Then I was faced with the dilemma of getting myself down to the hospital. I didn't have enough portable oxygen for Mama to make another trip to the city, and besides she was too tired to travel again. We might be at the hospital for hours or even a day or two. I needed to find a caretaker who was willing to come, on the spur of the moment, to stay with Mama for an indefinite time, here at our house where we had the big plug-in oxygen machine. Bless that dear lady who dropped everything she was doing and rushed over to help us. Even in the midst of tragedy there are small blessings.

Most of the family was at the hospital. We were just slogging through the nightmare.

".... brain dead ... "

".... organ donor ... "

Cheyenne, the only child, so loved, so lovely, lying there quietly as if she were the Sleeping Beauty, her forehead wrapped in gauze from the surgery that had attempted to save her young life, her long blond hair spilling down over her shoulders, her perfect skin, smooth, flawless. I held her hand. It was still warm...

Many hours later, a few of us stood around in the parking lot, talking quietly, feeling helpless. There really wasn't anything we could do. My son Tom said he would stay with his brother Ken as long as he was needed. I decided to get back home to Mama.

In the car on the way home, I realized that even though I hadn't had any sleep the night before, I wasn't tired. I was mad. Thinking about card number three, I was furious, in a rage. I started talking out loud, and then began yelling: "O.K. Are you satisfied now? Is this your number three? It wasn't enough taking my dear cat Jack, and then my only brother, Jim! Now you have to take my granddaughter Cheyenne, my son Ken's only child? Why? Why, you God-damned son of a bitch! Why?"

I wasn't sure who I was mad at. Was I mad at God? The Devil? Fate? The power behind those Tarot cards? Well, that sounds insane when you say it out loud, or even think it. Who, then? I didn't know. I started crying so hard that I had to pull the car over. I cried until I was wrung out, and then drove the rest of the way home. I hurried in my front door, greeted the caretaker, and went right over to my Mama. As I hugged and kissed her, I thought to myself, you can't have her yet, you... you whoever you are. The cards said three and you've already taken three from me. You can't have any more! Not yet! And then I heard what that voice was saying in my head, and another voice in another part of my head said, you've gone over the edge now Lynne. You are finally, certifiably, crazy.

Well, I may be a little crazy. But I try to take a step back and look at things as they really are. I try to take the bad with the good. I believe we all face tragedy and loss in this world, and that life can also be very unfair. The people who were involved in Jim's death and stole Mama's car and money were never prosecuted. The police knew who they were, habitual criminals, but they claimed Jim had loaned them the car and given them signed checks and credit cards to help them out, because they were "hard up." And the ex-boyfriend who killed my granddaughter was never brought to justice. Although he was a repeat offender of serious crimes, including felonies, and had been on probation at the time of his attack on Cheyenne, the court decided to try him as a minor, since he was a few weeks under the age of eighteen. He was released after a short sentence.

And so... we go on. Some people, trying to deal with the uncertainties of life, are helped by turning to horoscopes, fortune-tellers and Tarot cards. But as I said before, I'm not a superstitious person. I don't believe Tarot cards tell the future. I don't believe Tarot cards make people die. Nevertheless, I don't plan on having my cards read again.

Never, ever again.

HAMBURGER ANNIE

LIVING WITH MAMA

I remember when I was a very little girl, before I started school, Mama would take me with her to do errands. On our way home, we would stop at her favorite "hole in the wall" restaurant, as Mama called it, to buy hamburgers. Daddy used to tease her and call her Hamburger Annie, but she didn't seem to mind the nickname. She would just grin and say, "That's me!"

When we moved out of our apartment and into a house in the suburbs, Daddy bought a barbeque for the back yard so he could grill hamburgers for us. Mama said the burgers tasted so much better cooked over coals than they did fried in a skillet. And of course, they did!

Years later, after Daddy was gone and my brother Jim was living with Mama, I came to visit with her for the afternoon and then I went out to eat dinner with Jim in the evening. We went to a nice restaurant that specializes in hamburgers and I ordered the most delicious bacon-guacamole cheeseburger with French-fried onion rings and a chocolate malt. Yum! I still remember that meal fondly. As we were about to leave the restaurant, I said to Jim that we should bring back a cheeseburger for Mama, but he assured me that she wouldn't eat one from there. He had tried several times before, but she would only eat cheeseburgers from McDonalds.

When I brought Mama to live with me, one of the first things I did was to order her a cheeseburger from one of our nice local restaurants. I didn't eat meat anymore, but I didn't see why Mama couldn't enjoy a good cheeseburger. She took one bite, put it down disdainfully, and wouldn't finish it! Jim was right! She only wanted McDonald's cheeseburgers!

For the next several years, whenever we drove "off the hill," we would go to a McDonald's to buy Mama a cheeseburger. If we had guests coming up from the city, I would ask them to stop at the nearest McDonalds on their way up to see us and bring a cheeseburger for Mama. I can still remember the delight on her face when they came in the door, carrying a McDonald's sack, and she would say, "Oh, goody, you brought me a cheeseburger!"

Eventually the time came when Mama wouldn't even eat her favorite burgers. She would sip at her orange juice, take a swallow of her Ensure and nibble at a bit of buttered toast. I begged her to eat just another bite and pleaded with her to take just another sip.

Poring through my hospice literature about Diet For Elders, I came to the sad realization that Mama's body no longer needed the nutrition from food. Her body was shutting down. I cried heartbroken tears in my bedroom that night because I knew we were coming to the end of our time together. I was torn by conflicting feelings of not wanting to lose Mama and not knowing how long I could keep going on like this.

My little dog Annie hopped up on my bed with me, climbed onto my lap, and tried to lick the tears off my cheeks. As I sat there holding her, rocking back and forth, I told myself that I wasn't really losing Mama. She was going to a better place to be with Daddy and Jimmy and her own dear mother and father and brother. But she would still be here with me, too. Her loving spirit would always be here in these rooms. When I sat in her chair, or sipped tea from one of her favorite china cups, or looked at her picture, she would be with me. She would always be with me.

I'VE GOT TO BE GETTING BACK HOME

LIVING WITH MAMA

I sometimes feel a sense of something beyond this time and place, especially when talking with Mama at her bedtime. She is so frail now; she hardly eats any solid food and she sleeps pretty much around the clock most days. When I tuck her into bed at night, I often wonder if she'll still be with me in the morning.

We have our little routine: I help her into bed, put her slippers in just the right place, adjust her pillow, straighten her blanket, and put on her oxygen. Everything has to be just so. She even asks me to help her fold her Kleenex so it "looks just right." She's so sweet: thanks me for everything I do, tells me how much she appreciates my help, and compliments me on how pretty I am. Then I tell her that I must have inherited my good looks from my mother. I'm not sure she gets that little joke, but we both laugh. I kiss her goodnight and tell her I'll see her in the morning. She usually says, "O.K. honey, goodnight," but sometimes her response surprises me. She may tell me she's enjoyed visiting me, but needs to get home to fix her husband's dinner. Mama's been here with me for five years now, and Daddy's been dead for thirteen years. Not that it matters. Sometimes she tells me she plans to go to a peaceful, quiet place, and probably won't be here tomorrow.

Last night when I told her I'd see her in the morning, she took my hand and said quietly, "You know, honey, I've got to be getting back home to see my mother and dad. I've been gone such a long time, and they're wondering why they haven't heard from me."

What can I say to her? Despite her 87 years, she's a little child, worrying about getting home on time. So I told her, "Don't worry, Mama, you'll be able to go home soon, and I'm sure your folks know you're fine."

And I'm sure they do.

MOTHERLESS CHILD

Mama died last night. She slipped away quietly in her sleep. I am so very grateful that she went peacefully. I have prayed for that every day for the last few months. It's what all of us want at the end of our days, to slip away gently, in our own home, in our own bed, with the people we love around us—no pain, no fear, just peace.

I had a feeling Mama was going to go soon. She fell down in the kitchen last week, and she must have pulled a muscle in her back somehow, because for the last few days when she would sit up or lie back down, her back would hurt her a lot. I dosed her up with Ibuprofen, as much as I dared to give her, and she seemed comfortable if she was just lying still. But the more days that she spent in bed, the weaker she got, until she was unable to sit up alone, partly from weakness and partly because her back still caused her some discomfort.

Her last day she was hardly able to support any of her own weight, and I had to practically carry her to the bathroom and back. I was so afraid I would drop her. She only weighed about 90 pounds but that's way too much for me to handle: I'm not that much bigger than she is. I was so grieved for her, thinking of the prospect of her being bedridden and having to endure the indignity of diapers and bedpans and all that goes with that. My mother was such a lady, right up to the very last, and that would have been so hard for her. She accepted her loss of youth, health, and mobility with such grace and patience that she was an inspiration to all who knew her. I am so glad she was spared the loss of her dignity.

Night before last she called me in the middle of the night, but by the time I came downstairs, she had forgotten why she wanted me, and so she said as she often did, "I just wanted to tell you I love you, honey." Her little voice was just barely a whisper; she was so weak. I said, "I love you too, Mama, but you've got to stay tucked in your bed so you keep warm." She had been restless the last couple of days, which was very unusual for her, and had kicked off her blankets, which she rarely did. I didn't know that was going to be the last time I was able to tell her I loved her. I wish I had said, "I love you too, Mama," without saying "but."

Later that night, she called me downstairs again. She seemed a little anxious and took my hand and said, "You're not going to make me go away from here, are you?" I didn't even know what she meant by that, but she often said things that I didn't understand, and so I gave her a little hug and said, "You can stay here as long as you want to, Mama. You can stay here forever." I told her that, knowing that she probably wasn't going to be here with me much longer, but it seemed the right thing to say, because she gave me a little smile and said, "Oh, good, I'm so glad."

That was really our last conversation together. The next day she slept most of the day, and even when she was awake, she was not very responsive.

That evening, I said to a friend, "I was up with Mama several times last night. I can tell she's really tired today and I'm exhausted. I hope God is merciful and lets me sleep through the night tonight." As the old saying goes, "Be careful what you pray for." I'll regret those words forever.

I did get up once during the night to look in on her and make sure she hadn't kicked off her blanket. She was lying quietly in exactly the same position as she had been when I had tucked her into bed earlier, so I didn't go all the way into her room. I just went back to bed. In retrospect, I'm sure she was already gone then, because when I went in to her the next morning, her hands were already cold, gently holding the edge of her blanket. She looked so peaceful.

I sat on her bed and talked to her for a while, and cried, of course. I took off her pearl bracelet and her pearl cross necklace, and set them aside as gifts to give to my two daughters. Then I put her little gold watch on my wrist.

She used to ask me, "Is it ten after nine?" Sometimes it was, or sometimes it was a quarter of two. But she could still see the hands on that tiny little watch face! She just couldn't tell which was which. But Mama's in another time dimension now, another place with my dear Daddy, and my charming, handsome brother, and with her own beloved mother.

I used to sing an old, sad, folk song that went like this:

Sometimes I feel like a motherless child,
Sometimes I feel like a motherless child,
Sometimes I feel like a motherless child,
A long way from ho-o-ome, a long way from home.

Tonight, I am a motherless child.

MAY · 61 · ·

[Outside St. Timothy's Church]

MAMA, YOU LOOK SO PRETTY TODAY

LIVING WITH MAMA

It's been a little while since Mama's funeral, so I don't remember all the details, but that's O.K. It was a day of sadness and joy, but the joyful memories remain more and more clearly, and that's what I hold onto.

I wore my favorite dress that day, a long, soft, flowing dress of pale gray silk, with a small matching stole that looked as if it were crocheted from gossamer wings. And, of course, I wore Mama's little gold wristwatch, and also her pearl necklace.

When I came downstairs that morning, and looked for Mama in her favorite chair, which I always did and probably always will, I could almost hear her say with her sweet smile, "Oh honey, you look so pretty in that dress."

Later that day, I met family and friends at Saint Timothy's, a beautiful church with tall graceful spires and stained-glass windows. As a young girl, I sang there with my high school choir, was married in that church, and our babies were baptized there, too. Mama and Daddy were the godparents of all six of our children. Now as I waited near the baptismal font for family to arrive for the funeral, it seemed so appropriate to be remembering Mama in that very room, young and beautiful, holding our newborn baby in her arms.

In her funeral instructions, Mama had requested a closed casket, but when they wheeled in the light gray coffin, covered with a beautiful spray of pink roses, I wanted to see her for just a minute, one last time. And what a surprise! I don't know what I expected, but she looked so beautiful, it took my breath away. She was wearing a burgundy red dress with a lace collar and pearl buttons that I had bought for her one Christmas. It was her favorite dress. She always loved to have her hair and nails done, and her beautiful white hair and burgundy nail polish were fresh and pretty. And she still had her same sweet smile and peaceful expression. I touched her sleeve and said, "Mama, you look so pretty today." And she really did.

My four sons, two daughters, immediate family, and a few close friends were there for the service. I gave my girls, Cindy and Wendy, the pearl cross necklace and pearl bracelets that Mama had worn every day for years. Two of my sons, Tom and Michael, gave eulogies about their grama, telling funny stories and relating fond memories. I read a couple of the stories I had written about Mama, trying to say in a few minutes what we had shared together in a lifetime.

After the services were over, we went to our friends Dennis and Terri's house. It was a time of laughter and tears, gratitude, and pain. I think the pain was not just for losing Mama, but for all the losses we have had in our lives, for the people that weren't there that day, for the love that is lost, and for the emptiness that is left behind.

Late in the afternoon, some of us were outside on the patio. Dennis had built a wonderful roller coaster in their backyard, starting from a charming tree house tucked high up in an ancient maple tree, the track twisting and turning around the yard, coming to a screeching halt in front of the patio. My grandsons, Cindy's boys, were taking turns riding, squealing, and laughing, begging to be next in line. Then my daughters were coaxed and cajoled into riding, despite their reservations. The roller coaster was too small to carry the weight of the men, so I was next on the list. My excuses about having ridden it before and not feeling like it today were promptly dismissed, and before I knew it, I was climbing the ladder to the tree house, in my silk dress and high-heeled shoes, bracing myself for the ride in the brightly painted car, and flying through the air. As I put my arms above my head in the standard "no fear" position and whipped around the first curve, I looked up to the sky and thought, "Well, Mama, here I am on the day of your funeral, laughing and riding a roller coaster! And I know wherever you are, you're laughing with me."

I think Mama's life can be summed up in the words of my oldest son, Tom, spoken that day in church as he fondly remembered his grama: "From the earliest days of my childhood, I can remember my mother telling me about a picture of a baby boy that her mother kept on her desk at work, and how inquisitive clients would ask, 'Who is that cute little baby?' And she would quickly reply, 'That's my #1 grandson!'

["Tommy"]

At the time I wasn't sure if it meant I was the first, or I was the best. From the days of playing hide and seek in my grandparents' backyard, to driving my grama around in her brand-new Cadillac, I knew I was someone special in her life. I think in a grandmother's eyes, you can do no wrong, so I think it's up to us to live up to her expectations."

Mama made everyone feel like that. In her eyes, the ladies were all pretty, the gentlemen were all handsome, and I, her daughter, was, as she would tell all my friends, "one lovely lady." Those of us who loved her knew we were someone special in her life. We felt pretty. We felt handsome. We felt loved.

THE TEACUP

LIVING WITH MAMA

I told this story at Mama's funeral at the request of my daughters. Mama was so sweet and patient in her later years that my children liked to hear stories of how she was once young and feisty, and had a personality to go along with her red hair.

When Mama and Daddy got married, the Great Depression made for hard times. Although Daddy was fortunate to have a secure job with the post office, it was difficult for a young couple to afford the expense of setting up a new household. There was barely enough money for necessities, and none left over for extras, like new dishes, for example.

One day, standing in their kitchen, Mama and Daddy were having a "lover's spat," as arguments between newlyweds were so picturesquely described in those days. Mama became so exasperated with Daddy that she threw a teacup across the room at him. Despite the fact that the kitchen was very tiny, she missed him and the cup hit the wall and smashed to pieces. Instead of saying something practical like, "What are you doing; we can't afford to replace that cup," Daddy laughed at her and told her she "couldn't hit the broad side of a barn." She then proceeded to throw every cup, plate and bowl that was on the kitchen counter at him, as he continued to laugh at her.

I heard this story many years later. When I was fourteen, my mother went to work full-time. It was my responsibility to pick up my four-year-old brother, Jimmy, at kindergarten after school, walk home, and phone my mother at work to tell her we were home safely. I then had chores to do, and homework, and I learned to cook over the telephone, calling Mama to get instructions about food I didn't yet know how to prepare.

But the most difficult part of my job was caring for my little brother. Jim was a rascal all his life, but especially so for me, his teen-aged babysitter. He not only wouldn't do anything I asked him to do, but worse yet, he wouldn't stop doing things that he really shouldn't be doing.

One day I was so frustrated with him, and since I couldn't smack his little butt, which is what I felt like doing, I threw my hairbrush across the room. It hit the doorjamb and the handle broke off. When I showed it to my mother that evening, she smiled a little, and said, "Well you know, Lynne, you're going to have to buy a new hairbrush with your own money." Daddy overheard this conversation, and said, "Now Annie," he called her "Annie" when he wanted to tease her, "did you have to use your own money to replace all those dishes that you broke?" Mama actually blushed, and said, "Now Stephen, we don't have to talk about that in front of the children!"

But of course, he did!

A CELEBRATION OF LIFE

LIVING WITH MAMA

The fiddle swung into an Irish jig and toes started tapping around the room. Other instruments joined in: guitars, banjos, mandolins, whistles and bodhrans. Celtic music filled my log cabin and drifted out of the open doors and windows. My driveway and the usually quiet street out front were filled with cars. People milled about, sat in the log rockers on my front porch, and gathered in small groups. The murmur of conversation and quiet laughter filled the air. Inside, my kitchen table and counters were overflowing with what seemed like an endless assortment of delicious food, as every guest brought in one more dish to share. That day was a celebration of life, a mixture of joy and reverence, to honor and remember my dear Mama, an old-fashioned Irish Ceilidh. The word Ceilidh (pronounced Kaylee) means a home gathering of family, friends, food, storytelling, and music. What a perfect memorial for Mama; she enjoyed my friends and loved the music so much, and always went out of her way to tell my musician friends and music students how wonderful they sounded. I knew she enjoyed the music that day.

In the den adjoining the kitchen, I had set up a small table draped with my grandma's lace tablecloth and with a corkboard propped up behind it to display pictures of Mama at all stages of her life. The table held a collage of pictures and memorial cards for guests to take home, printed on my friend Sue's home computer. A large picture of Mama, printed and framed by my daughter Wendy, was flanked by Mama's crystal candlesticks holding tall, pale-blue candles. An album with a few of my short stories about our life together was there for guests to read. Flower vases, filled with pink roses and ferns left over from the funeral, were scattered throughout the house.

A guest book was available to record the feelings and memories of those who knew and loved my mother. One particular entry from one of Mama's caregivers seemed to capture with words the bond that existed between Mama and those whose lives she touched: "Thank you very much for having us work here, only it was not work, it was joy. I thank God for you and your mother. I have learned very much from both of you. Ann told me so many little stories of how she loved her brother; how he was handsome and kind. She told me all about how she was so happy and thankful to have had a good, kind family. I'm glad for her that she is with our Heavenly Father. I'm glad we will see her again."

I was hardly able to play my hammered dulcimer with my friends that day. My tears felt so close to the surface that they were ready to pour down my cheeks at the slightest provocation. I spent most of the day and evening visiting with my guests, some of whom I hadn't seen for a while. But when Barbara, the bass player with our string band, the Rose of Tejon, asked me to sing with her, I had to join in. The song we sang was one I always dedicated at our band performances to my Mama and Daddy, because they actually met at a country dance, and Mama, with her beautiful auburn hair, had been wearing a blue dress, all those many years ago. The song goes like this:

Oh, the night was clear, and the stars were shining,
And the moon came by, so bright in the sky.
All the people gathered 'round, and the band was tuning.
I can hear them now, playin' "Comin' through the rye."

She was dressed in blue, and she looked so lovely,
Just a simple flower, a small-town girl.
He took her hand and they danced to the music.
With a single smile, she became his world.

And they danced all night to the fiddles and the banjo-os.
Their lilting tune seemed to fill the a-a-air.
So long ago, but I still remember.
They fell in love at the Roseville Fair.

Now they courted well, and they courted dearly,
And they rocked for hours in the front porch chair.
Then a year went by from the time he told her,
"Will you be mine," at the Roseville Fair.

Now here's a song for all the lovers,
And here's a tune that you can share.
You can dance all night to the fiddles and the banjos,
The way they did at the Roseville Fair.

Where they danced all night to the fiddles and the banjo-os.
Their lilting tune seemed to fill the a-a-air.
So long ago, but I still remember.
They fell in love at the Roseville Fair.

I like to think that Mama and Daddy were dancing together that day, dancing to our music, at that celebration of life and love.

Song: Roseville Fair, written by Bill Saines

EPILOGUE

After Mama was gone, my youngest daughter Wendy and I went back to Ohio to visit relatives. Of all of my six children, Wendy is the one who most resembles Mama's side of the family, especially with her beautiful auburn hair, so it seemed appropriate that she should be the one who was able to make the trip with me.

I really felt the need to connect with family and renew my sense of where my people came from. Since both my parents and my only brother are gone, my only relatives of my generation or older are all "back East." It was so wonderful for me to visit with aunts, uncles, and cousins I rarely see. Everyone was so hospitable to us. We felt like visiting royalty: the planned family dinners that included nieces and nephews and their children too many for me to count, a tour around Mama's charming little hometown to visit the schools she attended, the church where she and Daddy were married, and the home she lived in as a child. With the help of a genealogy book, I discovered buildings in town where our ancestors had hardware stores and sold buggies and wood-burning stoves.

But my favorite part of rediscovering my roots was hearing the family stories about their long-ago adventures... or misadventures. My cousin Chris comes from a large family, and one day when she was explaining the connection between one of her aunts and my mother, she said, "By the way, did you ever hear the story of how my aunt Mary and your mother were both expelled from nursing college?"

Well, I almost fell off my chair laughing! My Mama? Who always got such good grades in school? My Mama who punished me for bringing home a C instead of A's and B's? Who lectured me about living up to my potential? Not MY Mama! I could hardly believe it!

I knew, or thought I knew, that she was a nurse before she and Daddy came to California. But it seems that Anna, as my Mama was called then, and her friend Mary had more than deviated from the rules of the nursing college. The final straw was the day they were instructed to take a corpse on a gurney to the morgue. The hospital was a large L-shaped building and their destination was on the farthest end. Since the shortest distance between two points is a straight line, the girls decided to take a shortcut. Out through the exit doors to the patio, and along the walkways through the garden they went. And I guess they got a little carried away speeding around corners because they careened off the walkway, tipped over the gurney, dumped the corpse into the rosebushes, and were unable to pick up the heavy body out of the thorns and brambles. Then along came whoever was in charge of rascally young nursing students and that was the end of their nursing career.

So, when as a young child, I asked Mama why she wasn't working as a nurse, she gave me some evasive answer about not being licensed to practice nursing in California. Well, I guess not! Apparently she wasn't licensed to practice anywhere on the planet!

In Loving Memory

Ann Dannemiller LaForge

OCTOBER 5TH, 1913 – AUGUST 19TH, 2001

CONTACT INFORMATION

Writing this book, though very emotional at times, has been a labor of love and, quite literally, a lifetime in the making.

I feel humbled and privileged to be able to share these experiences with you and hope you can relate to, understand, and empathize with what it takes to lovingly endure the obligations of being a caregiver to an elderly relative.

Any feedback or comments you may have would be most welcomed, and greatly appreciated. Please feel free to reach me at:

AmIYourMother.byLynne@gmail.com

With Love & Gratitude,
    Lynne

My dear friend and graphic designer, the source by which I was able to bring this book to fruition and the light of day, and to whom I am eternally grateful:

Keith Glaseman
CAGEY DESIGN
cageydesign@gmail.com

Made in the USA
Monee, IL
29 May 2024

58858494R00118